Mr. Erotica

By

Richard Jeanty

RJ Publications, LLC

Newark, New Jersey

The characters and events in this book are fictitious. Any resemblance to actual persons, living or dead is purely coincidental.

RJ Publications
richjeanty@yahoo.com
www.rjpublications.com
Copyright © 2010 by Richard Jeanty
All Rights Reserved
ISBN 0-9817773-2-0
978-0981777337

Printed in Canada

Octoberber 2010

1 2 3 4 5 6 7 8 9 10

ACKNOWLEDGEMENTS

I would like to thank all the important people in my life who have supported me through my writing career and other endeavors.

To my baby girl, Rishanna, I will always love you, unconditionally. I will never stop thanking you for making my days brighter and my life more beautiful. Also, Special "thanks" go out to my dad for his dedicated support.

Special thanks go out to all the book clubs and readers who continue to inspire me to keep writing. I would like to give a big shout-out to the street vendors and booksellers around the country and all over the world for keeping the world in tune with my literature. Thanks to all the book retailers and distributors who make it possible for my books to reach the people.

Special shout-outs go to all the New York book vendors and entrepreneurs. Special thanks to Hakim at Black and Nobel, Natty of African World Books, Max in Brooklyn, Marcus at Nubian Bookstore in Atlanta, Horizon Books; my main man Chris B and Grace in Brooklyn; Pogo and Ali in the Bronx; Henry, Mamabou and Ismael in

Harlem, and all the other stores and people that I cannot recall. My mind is crowded after finishing this book, but I appreciate all of you.

A big shout-out goes out to my nephews and nieces, as well as my brothers and sisters.

I would also like to thank my editor, Kerryn Sherod, for doing such a wonderful job with my book.

A special shout-out goes out to my assistant, Yolander Boston.

A special thanks to my fellow authors for keeping me on my grind.

Once again, I would like to dedicate this book to all the brothers and sisters who have forfeited their freedom justly and unjustly. Keep ya head up and keep the faith. Change is gonna come!

Introduction

Most of us grow up dreaming of having a family some day, but many of us have no idea what it takes to keep a family together. The reality is that far too many of us have experienced dysfunction and other obstacles that have ill-prepared us to have a family of our own.

The essence of a family can change the quality of life for anybody. Without a tight-knit family, there's no sense of belonging and there's always a lack of love and affection. In a fantasy world, it should be an easy dream to attain, but how can that be possible without a strong foundation?

I look at my baby girl everyday and I wish that I could wake up with her every morning and go to sleep with her every night, but that reality changed because the foundation of my relationship with my ex-wife was weak. Often times, we don't think a relationship is worth fighting for because of all the struggles and disagreement. It's so much easier to start on a new path, and sometimes it's justified. However, a new path means nothing if it continues to lead down the same road of destruction.

The question that I pose is "How hard are you fighting to keep your family together?" It's easy to want something, but are you man or woman enough to fight for it? We need to start keeping the family together for the sake of our kids and their future. It's time to be selfless!

Nostalgia

After our daughter was born, it seemed like my sex life was turned upside down. Marsha and I couldn't catch a break. Savant was a great baby most of the time, but she also did things like most babies would. She woke up at least once every night for feeding and my wife had to change her at least twice in the middle of the night. I was a proud daddy and a supportive partner for the most part, but my sexual needs weren't being satisfied. The fact that Marsha chose to breastfeed also played a big part in her lack of sleep at night, which affected my ability to get any ass at all during the day. She was tired most of the time and I felt like I was playing a game of cat and mouse with her in order to have sex. The fact that Marsha lost a good portion of the baby weight within six weeks after giving birth made it all the more difficult to resist her. Every time she walked by wearing those boy shorts she knows I love so much, I felt like taking a bite out of her ass. Then, I finally caught a lucky break.

This was the first time I was going to make love to Marsha in a long time. I had that hungry look in my eyes and she caught it; she knew I had been starving sexually and she looked a little frustrated herself. She needed to release. She had just rocked Savant to sleep and was eager to get started on dinner. Though my stomach was growling and in much need of some of Marsha's good cooking, I yearned for a different kind of food. Marsha's booty never looked so good as she strutted from the bedroom to the kitchen to tenderize the meat. She knew she shouldn't have walked by my office looking so sexy. I wanted, no, I *needed* to be selfish at that moment. I ran after her like a defensive back chasing a receiver to the goal line. Instead of tackling her, though, I brought her into the room and sat her on the loveseat in the corner. Marsha had never seen me act so aggressively. I pulled off her tube top and started playing with her nipples while we kissed passionately. My fire was burning and I needed her at that moment.

As my tongue took her breath away, my dick started to erupt. She timidly groped me and I was ready for some action. Her kisses had never felt better, and I didn't even bother to breathe as Marsha's tongue invaded my mouth in return. Her ass felt so plump and ripe as my hands caressed her cheek sensually. I missed my pussy and I needed to taste her. I spread Marsha's legs open across the loveseat so I could begin the raid of her pussy with my tongue. *Mmm, mmm, good* was all I could say as I stared at her pinkness. It felt like I was seeing it for the first time. Marsha hadn't had time to shave like she normally did, so her terrain was a little hairy. I used my fingers to brush aside her pubic hair so I could part her pussy lips in order to savor her clit in my mouth. She held on for dear life because Marsha knew that I could eat her pussy well. As I extended my tongue to rub it over her clit, we could hear Savant crying loudly in her room and she always took precedence over everything – and I mean everything. Marsha's flame immediately flickered and I was left with a hard dick in my hand and an unsatisfied appetite in my office.

I really wanted to take care of it myself, but I felt dirty having to jerk off while my wife was taking care of my baby girl in the next room. I simply allowed my dick to go to sleep as I refocused my energy on the latest book I was working on.

A New Life

I still hadn't gotten off the high from my last book; the response from my readers and the wonderful reviews from the critics reinforced my confidence and gave me the adrenaline rush I needed to produce a best-seller. Also, looking at my baby girl while she slept in her crib helped keep me focused and on track to maintain my status in the writing game. She's the best muse I could've asked for.

Soon after Marsha's divorce was finalized, we got married. She officially became Mrs. Richardson and my daughter's last name was also changed to Richardson. We had the most wonderful wedding with 150 of our closest friends and family. My uncle couldn't believe that I was getting married at such a young age, but he could also see the happiness that Marsha brought to my life. He was the one who provided us with a pastor for the ceremony which was at the Park Plaza hotel in Boston. Our families and friends got a chance to mingle and it was a wonderful event. Rammell couldn't help being himself. We caught him acting like he was the meat between a sandwich of two women on the dance floor.

Marsha had a hard time figuring out which of her friends she wanted to invite to her wedding. Since I had slept with all of them courtesy of her, she was reluctant about having them around her future husband. At the end of the day, I gave her the confidence and comfort she needed by telling her, "Baby, you know I was on the clock with every single one of those women when I slept with them. They each had the opportunity to snag me if I wanted them, but I wanted you. I fell in love with you because you were the one I wanted, not them." She smiled after hearing my statement and said, "You're right baby, I'm gonna show those heifers that you are my man and they can only dream about your dick from now on. I'm inviting every single one of them." I was laughing because Marsha managed to find humor in the situation.

As I sat at the table staring into my daughter's and wife's eyes, I saw nothing but a happy future and marital bliss for years to come. I can't describe the emotions that I was experiencing, but it felt good. Even though Savant was still a toddler, I decided to have a special dance with my daughter at the wedding. My mother and Marsha's mother kept her busy through the ceremony. At the end of it, I was glad everyone had a great time at the wedding.

I didn't pay too much attention to Marsha's friends at the wedding as I was focused on her. However, I heard that Rammell ended up getting head from one of the housewives while her husband got piss drunk and another wife got a quickie from Kevin in the bathroom. I'm not sure if they were rumors, but I would never put anything past those housewives. Besides, there was no reason for Rammell and Kevin to tell me things that were untrue. Men are worse than women sometimes when it comes to their sexual encounters. A sexual experience is not great until we share it with a friend, except of course, when it involves our wives.

The Sexual Exploits at My Wedding

According to Kevin, "Big jugs Becky," as he called her, was not wearing any panties when she lured him into the women's bathroom for a quickie. She flashed one of her big breasts to Kevin as he was walking to the men's room with a Heineken in his hand and trying not to pee on himself. She then followed with her index finger motioning for him to come towards her. She had been paying attention to Kevin all night as he put his dance moves on some of the female guests on the dance floor. The fact that Kevin managed at least a six pack of Heineken within an hour at the reception, helped to loosen him up with the ladies. Becky's imagination must've gone wild as she saw the gyrating waist of Kevin caressing the hips of the sisters to the rhythm of the Hip Hop beat. Kevin was the best dancer of all of us. Not only was he a bad boy, he also danced like one. Many of the women at the party already knew who he was because of the success of his first street novel, *The Game is Mine*, which I published under my publishing company, Stories R Us.

Feeling like a celebrity, Kevin was dancing the night away and lining up women for later that night in the process. Though his book was primarily about the "street life," Kevin's edgier sex chronicles found their way to the pages of his book and the women were more than eager to learn if his imagination really pushed the sexual limits in real life. There was one scene about a man fucking this woman in the middle of a hallway, and that scene kept the female readers asking for more. And even his male readers had to give him props on a job well done. Becky's silicone-filled titties were hard as a rock, but they looked perky to Kevin as her nipples protruded through the silk dress she was wearing. "You got some moves there, handsome," she said to Kevin. "Oh yeah? How about you show me some of your moves?" Kevin said as he backed her up into the bathroom. He stood directly behind the bathroom door to keep any intruder from entering, while he dropped his pants to his ankles and his ten-inch dick was sticking up, ready to invade Becky's pussy. But first, Kevin realized he hadn't peed yet and he really needed to before he got started with Becky. Kevin, a little inebriated, found himself peeing on everything except the toilet. "Are you ok in there?" Becky asked as she heard the full strength of Kevin's piss hitting the bathroom wall and the floor. The women's bathroom was a complete mess by the time Kevin was done.

Still undeterred by the mess Kevin made in the stall, Becky was ready to take his dick in her mouth as he repositioned himself by the door. "Let's move over near the sink," she suggested, so they could have more room and comfort. "Nah, I want to stand by the door so no one can get in," he said to her. "I already locked the door, silly," she confirmed. Kevin started laughing because he hadn't noticed the lock on the door. "Well, let's do this then," he said as he grabbed his dick and directed her mouth to it. Becky happily squatted down, holding her dress up to keep it from hitting the floor, while the other held Kevin's dick as she wrapped her lips on the shaft of it to experience his ten inches of pleasure. "Your cock is beautiful and big," she said between licks. Kevin's face was gleeful as Becky's thin lips and smooth tongue went up and down and around his dick. The blowjob would go on for about five minutes until Kevin pulled her up to him to suck on her fake titties. Realizing that her titties looked better than they tasted, Kevin moved on to her wet pink pussy, filling every inch of it with his fingers after lifting up her long dress. He soon bent her over the sink, lifted her dress and penetrated her from behind. Never one to leave his house without a condom, Kevin wrapped himself in a Lifestyle extra sensitive before he commenced the pussy assault.

With a hand full of bleached blond hair, Kevin pounded Becky's pussy from behind. "Fuck me with that big black cock," she kept whispering like a porn star. "You love this black dick, huh?" Kevin asked as he fucked her with rage. "Yes! Fuck me! I love your cock!" she screamed in a low tone. Kevin wrapped his hand around her neck as he tried to split open her pussy with his big dick. The more forceful he got with her, the more excited she became and the more she wanted him to fuck her. "Oh my gosh! This is what I call fucking!" Becky exclaimed. Kevin was laughing inside because he knew that he was fucking this white woman the way that a former slave would exact revenge on a plantation owner's daughter.

Kevin turned Becky around and sat her on the sink. He brought her ass to the edge of the sink as he inserted his entire dick inside her. Becky couldn't keep her eyes closed as she moaned in ecstasy. A few minutes later she was holding on for dear life as Kevin made her cum like she never came before on the bathroom sink. Becky didn't want Kevin to leave unsatisfied. "I want you to fuck me in the ass," she suggested. The suggestion alone had Kevin damn near busting a nut before he even penetrated her. Kevin had never had anal sex before. It was new and exciting territory to him. Becky's asshole wasn't as tight as he imagined, but he was still excited none the less. Watching his dick moving in and out of Becky's ass with ease was a thrill and he soon shouted, "I'm coming!" She turned around, pulled his condom off, and took his dick down her throat to suck every drop of semen from his dick.

Becky and Kevin never saw the two female spectators standing by the last stall in the bathroom. "I'm next!" one of them yelled. "No, I'm next!" the other one exclaimed. "Ladies, there's enough of me to go around. How about a threesome in my room later on?" he suggested as he handed them a spare key to his room with the room number on the card. The two obviously good friends, agreed to meet Kevin in his room after the reception.

Rammell's account of his sexual tryst was no less exciting. According to him, the young slim and petite brunette started smiling at him while he was lounging in the lobby after coming off a long stint on the dance floor with her. He wasn't thinking that it was nothing more than a dance, but she enjoyed his moves so much, she followed him to the lobby for more conversation. "Are you from Boston?" she asked with a tempted grin. "Yes, I'm from Mattapan," Rammell told her. No names were exchanged, but they somehow found themselves stuck in the elevator on the tenth floor and the brunette was servicing Rammell like he had never been serviced before. It started with a flirtatious comment about Rammell's bulging crouch while they were dancing. "Were you happy to be dancing with me or did you have a roll of quarters in your pocket?" she asked playfully. "A pack of quarters are far smaller than what you felt, and I was a lot harder than that," he retorted. "How about you show me how hard you are and what kind of roll you're packing?" she assertively told him. "The pleasure would be all mine," Rammell told her.

After searching around for any sign of a camera, Rammell and the brunette started making out in the elevator as they made their way up. By the time they reached the tenth floor, the urge to pull the "emergency stop" button couldn't be contained. The brunette grabbed a hold of Rammell's nine-inch dick and took it in her mouth with a big smile. She slobbed on it until it could get no harder. They knew that management would soon come to their rescue as the alarm continued to go off, so Rammell tried to rush a quick nut before the doors could be opened. He started humping her mouth very quickly until semen started oozing out of his dick and into the back of her throat, as he was holding on to her head. "Oh shit! I'm coming!"

- 18 -

Rammell hissed as the white, thick substance exited his penis. "I want it all down my throat," the brunette said while squeezing it all out of Rammell's dick.

Before maintenance could force open the elevator door, Rammell had released the emergency button and the brunette had wiped her mouth clean with a napkin. Both got off of the elevator to walk back to the reception with Rammell feeling a little light on his feet and more jovial than usual.

Their sexual trysts remind me of the fun that I had with Marsha's friends when I was a gigolo. I could only smile when my boys told me their little stories. If only they knew what I had been doing a few months prior to my wedding day. They would go nuts with envy.

My Family

There is a reason why I enjoy doing what I do. The gratification I get whenever I release a book that's catapulted to the top of the New York Times' best-seller list within a week is exciting. I especially like the long lines that form around the corner at every bookstore I visit while people wait to get their books signed. What I do is fun and I wouldn't have it any other way. But my wife has been on my back lately, talking about, "You don't spend any time with the family. You're constantly writing and that's all your life is about." Well, if I don't write these books, she won't be able to live that luxurious lifestyle she enjoys so much. She has no idea the pressure I'm under whenever I have to write a new book. The minute one of my books flops, my publisher will move on to the next hot author. With so many talented writers out there penning within the same genre I do, I have to make sure I stay on top of my game. A few months after I self-published my first novel, I was approached by a major publisher that offered me a mid-six figure deal for three books. It was a decision I pondered for quite some time. I hate the pressure of having to meet a deadline. My personal story, *The Bedroom Bandit*, did well with my growing audience while published under my own company. However, it was my second book, *The Nympho Within*, that gained me national fame. This was the epic of the personal battle for this young lady trying to overcome a sexual addiction. Women fell in love with the main character, but most of all, they fell in love with the erotic scenes that filled most pages of the book.

My wife is just gonna have to get used to the fact that I work hard to provide for my family. With three kids, a multi-million dollar home, a Mercedes truck, a 750 BMW and a vacation home in the Cayman Islands, I have no time to rest. Not only that, my wife has expensive taste and she's rearing my children the same way. I should've never given her the option to become a homemaker after our first child -- I'd created a monster.

Even though I had started my own publishing company, I had decided to sell the rights to my first book to a major house because my uncle advised me to do so. The deal also included a second book. That deal put me in a position to brand my name on a national level and also help the new, up-and-coming authors who were signed to my own company. The deal made sense and I took it at the time. I don't regret the decision because I'm a hustler and I know how to sell myself.

My wife and I never planned on having a third child, but the baby came and we have to deal with it. He's the most precious of all my kids and the only boy. Don't get me wrong I love my two girls, but my baby boy is my heart. I treated my girls the same way when they were born. However, there's something so special about a little boy and his dad. My daughters bring life into me, but my son makes me want to challenge life. Every man wishes he gets a son, and I'm no different. Whenever my wife is bickering at me, I find solace in the company of my babies. "Can you read to me, daddy?" Savant would say with one of her favorite books in her hand. My daughter is the only child that I have who seems to be interested in reading and writing at an early age. She mimics everything that I do. She'd see me writing on a notepad; then she'd reach for a pen and a piece of paper to do the same. She especially enjoys playing with my computer. She enjoyed it so much, I had to give her a computer of her own at two years old. I got tired of her deleting my work by accident, so I had no choice. She knew how to turn on the computer and how to turn it off. And she would call me over to open a blank document so she could type whatever it was that she wanted to type. My daughter's a trip and I love her to death.

I named my son Joseph after my uncle Joe. I didn't want him to carry a name that was meaningless and my father's name has not been something that I felt was worth passing on. I have a little trooper, though. He got me a few times while changing his diaper. He peed right into my face, as if he was waiting for me to unfasten the diaper so he could say, "I got you!" He even pooped in the water once when I was trying to give him a bath in the tub, but I let his mother take care of that stinky mess. That's my boy! He has a personality all his own. He has this mysterious stare when he wants to be picked up and most of the time I feel like I'm forced into it. My girls just adore their little brother. It's going to be hard to keep a balance among the children. Savant stole my heart and my daughter, Daniella, named after my mother, is the most caring and sweet little girl in the world. Daniella is the most affectionate of the three children and she plays no favoritism between me and her mother. When she wants to play with daddy, she's focused on me, and when she wants to be with her mother she's focused on her. Since she's the middle child, I don't ever want her to be left out and I'm making a conscious decision to ensure that never happens.

My wife has been nothing short of great since the arrival of our children. I try as much as I can to help out with the kids, but this lady does the best balancing act of homemaker, lover, mother, homey, and friend that I have ever seen. I get overwhelmed easily when I'm in the presence of all the children, but my wife acts like she has a third eye or peripheral vision at all times. She catches things that I'm amazed she's able to catch. One time Daniella thought it would be amusing to drink from the toilet bowl, while I was changing Joseph's diaper. I didn't even notice she was gone until my wife brought her to me with her shirt completely wet because she had obviously been playing in the toilet bowl in the half bath located on the first floor. I can't wait to tell her the stories on how she drank toilet water as a child. My wife always made it a point to keep the toilet super clean since Daniella liked to sneak into the bathroom.

The children have also brought our sex life to a standstill. My wife and I are lucky if we can get it on once a month when we used to have sex damn near every day. It's been tough on me but I understand that my wife is tired most of the time because of the kids. The baby is too young to pack up and send to my mother or her mother's house so we can spend some time alone. The fact that my wife is so overprotective of her only son, plays a big role in us having no "alone" time. I've been doing what I've needed to do to release the tension as of late. Once the kids are sleeping and my office door is closed, I pull out a bottle of my favorite Keri lotion, log on to my favorite porn site and it's me and *Palm*ela going at it until I reach the sky.

My wife gives the best head and I almost feel guilty asking her for it because she looks so tired most of the time. To be truthfully honest, I wouldn't mind having head occasionally without the sex. She knows just what to do to get me there quickly with her tongue. However, I feel like I'm being selfish if I make any kind of sexual suggestion to my wife. I tried talking to her about it, but she told me that the kids took away most of her strength by the time I'm ready to have her. I've been looking for the right time when she hasn't exhausted all her strength with the kids, but I'm not a good time keeper. I even feel guilty when we have sex because she doesn't seem to be enjoying it anymore because of fatigue. Marsha knows that I love sex and she promised that we will have a sex life again in the near future, but I'm a horny man.

Hitting The Road

My new book was finally released a few weeks later and I had to hit the road to start promoting it. Once again, the book received great reviews across the board from newspapers to magazines to book clubs. It was refreshing to hit the road again. I made a promise to my wife that I would only travel from Thursday thru Sunday and that I would be home early enough on Sundays for dinner. I knew I was going to miss my family, but somebody had to put food on the table. I always get excited about my tour because it gave me a chance to interact with my readers. I especially enjoy the meetings with the book clubs. Every reader that I meet is important to me and their feedback is appreciated. Being a new writer, I needed as much constructive criticism as I could get and I never turned sour on anyone because of a bad review.

My first stop on the tour was Fort Lauderdale, Florida. I was at the Borders store located at the Aventura mall when she walked in. Her petite body was to die for. My estimated guess had her standing at 5ft 3 inches tall, 34 C-cup breast, a 24-inch waist and 38-inch hips. I had been with enough women to know the different sizes. She was light-skinned with long flowing hair and she wore a short, white linen dress, red pumps with 5-inch heels, a red Chanel handbag and a pair of Chanel shades. All I could say was "Wow," when I laid eyes on this woman. The person standing in front of me must have thought that "wow" was meant for her because she started giggling uncontrollably like a child. She was cute, but I was lost in the stranger with the white dress. The mystery lady was headed straight toward my table as if she knew me. I gave her a welcoming smile as I intently paid attention to her without realizing the giggling lady was still standing in front of me with her book in hand still waiting for me to sign it. I quickly noted the frustration on the faces of the people who were waiting in line, so I grabbed the lady's book and signed it. I could tell that she knew that I noticed her even though she was toward the back of the line waiting with what appeared to be a copy of my second book in her hand. Subconsciously, I increased the speed of my penmanship so I could get to the mystery woman sooner rather than later. At that point, her reason for being there was all that mattered to me. I wanted to know what she had to say about my new book, *Doggy Style*.

I was excited about *Doggy Style* because the book chronicles the life of three friends who faced the tough decision of settling down in Atlanta. With men being outnumbered almost thirteen-to-one by women, most brothers are forced to play the field longer than they want to in that city. Add the homosexual and down-low brothers to the mix and you have a city full of frustrated black women who get played daily because of the lack of men. "A good man is so hard to find," should be the motto in Atlanta. I wanted to write a book that deals with the frustration that so many professional, beautiful sisters have to deal with while shedding light on the fact that boys will always be boys. I wanted that book to be my homage to the struggling single scene for women in that chocolate city.

The mysterious woman's physical beauty almost seemed to fit the perfect description of one of the characters that I wrote in my book. The character was a professional entertainment lawyer who got treated like crap by men in the entertainment industry. Because of her status as an attorney, she was always accosted by athletes and entertainers who didn't seem to appreciate her worth. She grew frustrated with them and vowed to bring them all down. It was a fun character to write because she got revenge on all her abusers.

Anyway, "Ms. Thang" finally made her way to the front of the line and I could instantly inhale the sweet aroma of her Chanel No.5 perfume. If I had to guess, I would say she was a big fan of Coco Chanel's designs. "Hi, how are you doing today?" I said to her jovially. Everyone around looked at me all strange like I had committed a crime. And then suddenly I could hear the jealous whispers. "You ain't greet nobody else like that. I guess I need to be wearing a tight-ass skirt to get a special greeting," one lady said. I guess I didn't realize my faux-pas until it was too late. There was no come back to the lady's comment, so I said nothing. "I'm fine," the lady finally answered after she allowed the catty women to make their smart-ass comments. "I won't be taking much of your time. I just wanted to come down and tell you how much I appreciate your work and your latest book is the bomb," she said before walking away. I was thinking, "is this all I get?" Just as fast as she came, she was gone. I didn't even get to sign her book. She wasn't even interested in my autograph.

After my signing that Friday, I went home thinking about how fine the mysterious woman was. I had used my imagination to bring to life the most gorgeous woman that I had ever created, but this was the real thing. I never fathomed that a woman could be this fine. Of course, I think Sanaa Lathan is one of the most beautiful women in Hollywood, but that's Hollywood and it's expected. However, this woman was real and drop dead gorgeous. Before I got lost too much into this woman, I decided to pick up the phone to touch base with my wife. I had never cheated on my wife since we got married and I didn't want to start.

"Hi baby," her sweet voice echoed through the receiver after picking up the phone. There was a time when the sound of my voice could send a stream down my wife's panties, and I wondered if I was still doing it. "Are your panties wet right now? Because my dick is definitely hard from hearing your sweet voice," I said to her. "Boy, I ain't got time to be getting wet with these three kids running wild around the house." My wife once again shut down the idea of my fantasy with her. I was hoping we could have a little phone sex to help make my night go a little easier. Again, I needed to be a supportive husband, so I said nothing negative about the situation. "How are my babies doing?" I asked switching the conversation to something that she would be more in tune with. "The kids are fine. I took them to the park today and they had a ball," she told me. My wife always got excited about her children. She was definitely the best mom, and I appreciated her for it. "Can I say hi to them?" I asked. She took the phone and held it to my oldest daughter's ears. "Hi boo-boo. It's daddy," I whispered on the phone to my daughter. "Hi, daddy. I miss you," she said excitedly. My daughter learned to speak by the time she was two years old and she's very sweet and expressive. "I miss you to, baby. Daddy's coming home soon and we're gonna play all our favorite games. Are you helping mommy with your sister and brother?" I playfully asked her. She also likes to play the role of big sister and does a great job trying to give my wife a hand with her siblings. "I helped mommy feed my brother. We went to the park. We played hop scotch...." She was ranting about everything and I could hear her mother in the background telling her to give her back the phone. I told my daughter I loved her. I also told my wife to hold the phone to the ears of my younger kids so I could tell them I love them. I hung up the phone reassuring my wife and family that I love them and they were number one to me.

A New Day

I never anticipated a second visit by the stranger. This time she was the first one waiting to see me at the Borders located on Dixie Highway in Miami. This time she was also wearing a hot little red dress that contoured her very curvaceous body. She was wearing high heel open toe pumps and a small red bag in her hand. Lady in red was killing them. I got the feeling that she knew the kind of effect she wanted to have on me before she left her house. Only a fool or a gay man would not notice such a sexy, beautiful woman. Instead of allowing her to wait in line like everybody else, I approached her to speak to her individually. "Please tell me that you missed me, that's why you're back today," I said sarcastically with a smile on my face. "You would be so lucky. I decided to come by to get your new book for my book club because it's our book of the month. I wanted them signed individually to each member. I thought it would be kind of special for my club to have autographed copies," she said dryly. I wanted to say, "Excuse me," but I chilled. She handed me a list with twenty names of the book club members and I signed each book for her. I was happy that she bought so many books, but I wanted to know a little more about this mysterious woman. Could she have been a stalker with ulterior motives? I wondered. Against my better judgment, I decided to forgo my own personal thought about her as I wished to bask in her beauty alone, even for ten minutes over coffee.

When I finally got to the last book that I was autographing for her, I decided to say something unusual and abnormally unbecoming of me. "Do you want to meet for coffee in a couple of hours?" I asked her under my breath so the other people in line wouldn't hear me. "Why, do you want to get to know me better?" she asked sarcastically. I didn't know what to say, so I said nothing. "You're obviously married because you have your wedding ring on, but you want to have to coffee with me. Do you think your wife would mind you being in the company of such a hot woman?" she continued with her sarcasm. She definitely wasn't lying about being hot, but I had to say something quick before things got out of hand. "I'm sorry, you're right. I was outta line for even suggesting that we should have coffee. Thanks for your support and I hope your book club enjoys the read," I said almost feeling sorry for myself. "Wow! I didn't peg you as the kind of man who would give up so easily. Did my mentioning your wife affect your decision to have coffee with me?" she said in a teasing manner. By now she was obviously holding up the line and the people behind her were growing a little impatient. "Since you're putting me in a compromising position, you might as well feed me and I might entertain the idea of allowing you into my space. How about you meet me at Joe's Stone Crab restaurant in a couple of hours after your signing? I'm sure you know how to look it up on your Blackberry, right?" she said before walking away with the twenty books stacked in her hand exposing her defined biceps. I didn't even get a chance to say anything to her. This woman was confident that I wouldn't stand her up.

My signing went well as usual and I was grateful that so many people came out to support me. Now I had to deal with Ms. Thang whose name I didn't even know. What did she expect me to go walk around a restaurant looking for her without a name? I contemplated not showing up, but this woman was not your everyday woman. I needed to know what the hell was up with her. As a writer, I'm a little more inquisitive than most people, and I get intrigue by eccentric characters when I meet them. They are the people that can make a story very interesting and I wanted to learn more about the mysterious lady because she would be a great character to write about.

Are We On A Date Or What?

I couldn't believe that I was going through the browser on my G1 phone to find the address to this restaurant. People always make the assumption that I carried a Blackberry, but I find the G1 to be more convenient and efficient, just my personal opinion. I was finally able to locate the restaurant on Washington Avenue in Miami Beach thanks to the GPS in my rental car. I was there about thirty minutes after my signing. I didn't want to appear too anxious, but I was. I wasn't anxious about the mysterious woman's beauty so much as I was eager to learn about her character. She seemed bold, assertive and completely in control. I had never written about a woman like that and I wanted to find out more. I'm very certain that my wife would probably be upset that I decided to meet a strange woman for dinner, but sometimes I have to go farther for better research.

Finding Ms. Thang was a lot less difficult than I anticipated. The hostess at the restaurant couldn't stop staring at the beautiful woman dressed in red who had walked in a few minutes before I did. In fact, most of the people in the restaurant were trying to catch glimpses of her as if she were a movie star. Just the mention of her outfit to the hostess alone helped to point me in the right direction. "Excuse me, I'm meeting someone here, perhaps you might've seen her. She's wearing a red dress..." Before I could even finish my sentence, the hostess offered to walk me right over to the mysterious woman's table. "Sir, follow me. I think I know exactly who you're looking for," she said with a smile. I wondered if the hostess was trying to catch another up close and personal glimpse of this gorgeous woman because she was ardent to walk me over to her.

I couldn't help notice this woman was looking as stunning as ever as she applied her lipstick while I made my way to her table. For the first time since we met, I finally got to experience her pleasant, beautiful smile. She had the most perfect white teeth and this glow emanated from her when she exposed her pearly whites to me. I knew that I would have to proceed with caution or I would lose my grip on the situation. I smiled back to acknowledge her. My number one defense mechanism at this point became my wedding band. I wanted to hold it up and expose it as much as I could so this woman knew that there wasn't going to be any line crossed. "Have you been waiting long?" I asked after pulling out my chair to sit down. "I got here a few minutes before you did. I ordered a drink, would you like one?" she asked politely. I definitely needed a drink, so I waved the waiter over to ask for my favorite Kamikaze on the rocks. That Chanel No. 5 perfume she was wearing definitely made it hard for me to concentrate. I decided to make small talk so she wouldn't notice her affect on me. "So what did you order to drink?" I asked. "Just a Martini, I like them," she said. "Ok, that's an interesting drink. Did you get it shaken or stirred?" I commented in a comedic way hoping to show my lighter side. "You got jokes," she said. It soon hit me that I had been referring to this woman as mysterious and strange since I met her. I needed to know her name. When I signed all those books for her, she wasn't specific as to who she was on the list of names.

I didn't want the situation to turn awkward so I decided to ease in my inquiry about her name. "I know that you know my name because it's written on the cover of my books, but you never told me yours," I said to her with a smile on my face. "I guess you're not as perceptive as I thought. My name was at the top of the list I handed you for my book club," she said to me. Honestly, I didn't remember any of those names and I wasn't about to play some guessing game. "Well, how about you help a brother out? I've been signing books for the last couple of hours and it would be hard to remember everybody's names," I told her. "I simply don't recall anybody in that line picking up twenty copies of your book at once. I should be special and my name should be the only name that you remember at all," she said trying to bust my chops. I guess she had a point, but I didn't want to argue with her. "You're right. I still would like to know your name, though, if we're gonna be having dinner together," I said trying to be charming.

My drink arrived a few minutes later and Ms. Thang was already done with her first drink. She ordered another and another and another one, until our food arrived. She must've had four drinks before dinner. I saw no dilating pupils, no slurred speech and she was more alert than ever. However, I did notice that she was starting to relax a little more. The food looked great and I couldn't wait to bite into my lobster tail. She ordered king crabs with mashed potatoes and salad. Her food looked delicious as well, and I sort of wished that I could taste it, but that would have been overstepping my boundaries. I left it alone. "My name is Kendra," she said to me out of the blue in between bites of her crab. I could tell right away that crab was her favorite seafood and she had no problem breaking the hard shell to get the meat out. The way she savored that crab meat was reminiscent of one of the housewives having her way with my dick. I had never seen crab meat eaten so seductively. "Kendra is a pretty name. It suits you," I said in a complimentary way while taking small bites of my lobster.

Dinner was going along fine when Kendra all of sudden asked me, "Why are you here? I'm sure your little wife would be fuming if she saw you sitting there across from me admiring me like most of these men in here. However, you should consider yourself lucky because I'm very particular about the company I keep." How do you come back from a statement like that? I was speechless and I remained so until I finished eating my food. I'm sure she was smiling inside because she thought she had pulled my card. I finally allowed my thoughts to marinate long enough to muster the courage to give her an answer. "Actually, my intentions before I came here were to basically get a better understanding of you as a woman. Obviously, you're not typical and you know it. So I find women like you intriguing and as a writer, I need to make sure that I keep the variety as a spice in my novels. Why have you come to see me twice?" I retorted. I knew she didn't think she was just gonna check me like that and get away with it. Hell yeah she was beautiful, but so is my wife. I just knew that her demeanor and approach was unusual and I wanted to see what it was all about. At that point, I had already made up my mind that I was gonna leave her sooner rather than later to drive back to my hotel after dinner.

"I've come to see you twice because I wanted to meet you in person. I wanted to meet the man who has the ability to make me cum while simply reading his words. I wanted to know how you are so in touch with the female body. What did you do in your past life to know so much on how to please a woman?" she asked out of thin air, then continued, "Maybe the *Bedroom Bandit* was not fiction at all." I never quite dubbed myself a sexual expert, but I was willing to give her a satisfactory answer. "Well, women are not as difficult as they want to make it appear. If a man pays close enough attention to a woman, he should have no problem pleasing her. However, the problem is that most men think that all women are the same. They think what works for Jane is gonna work for Mary. I'm not like that and that is why I stand above the rest," I told her. "You're a cocky bastard, aren't you?" she commented. "Did you want the truth or a humbling lie?" I asked. "I like your honesty and I believe that you are the character that you wrote about," she said while allowing her beautiful smile to re-emerge. "Why can't I just be a writer who uses my imagination to entertain my readers?" I gave her something to ponder for about a minute or two. "You want me to buy that you're just a writer, right? You've never been a bedroom bandit rummaging through the upscale streets of Boston tearing up every piece of ass willing to pay for your services, huh?" she said sarcastically. I tried to keep a straight face when she made that comment, but I couldn't.

I never confirmed anything for her. She decided to have one more drink before we left the restaurant. Her tolerance for alcohol was higher than most women, but it also made her more flirtatious and playful. I paid for dinner and as we were walking out of the restaurant, I asked, "Do you need a cab home?" She smiled before answering my question, "Why would I need a cab home when I can get a ride from my favorite, handsome author? You're driving, aren't you?" she asked with curiosity. I almost wanted to lie to her, but I confirmed that I was driving. "You didn't drive down here, did you?" I asked wondering if she might have parked her car somewhere near the restaurant. "No, I didn't drive. I had my girlfriend drop me off because I knew I was gonna be going home with you," she said matter of factly. "Wow!" was all I could say. Did she really think that I was that easy? What made her think that I would cheat on my beautiful wife? All of a sudden, I started thinking about my babies at home and my wife lying next to me in my beautiful bed at night enjoying each other's company. I gave no response to her comment. "I need your address so I can put it on the GPS," I said to her. At that point, I was guarded and she could feel it. I said very little as I hopped on 395 north toward 95 north heading to her house in Boca Raton.

There was silence in the car for a while before she said, "You mean to tell me that you're a man who writes the steamiest stories that I have ever read, and you are faithful to your wife?" Her question was a little weird, but I gave her a satisfactory answer. "I value my wife and my family, so I know how to use my brain instead of my dick when I make decisions that can affect my family," I told her. "Bravo," she said as she started clapping. I kept my eye on the road and continued to drive. I couldn't wait to drop this lady off at home. "Are you telling me you don't wanna suck on my luscious tities and fuck my plump ass because you love your wife and kids? You know how many men I've been with who love their wife and kids? I don't wanna marry you. I might want you to fuck me on the kitchen counter the way you fucked Tara," she said. By then, I knew it was the alcohol talking, so I just ignored her comment.

Finally, we reached her beautiful stucco home located on a street lined with palm trees in an upscale subdivision, which made me wonder what she did for a living. The home looked spacious from the outside alone. I could only imagine what the interior must've looked like because Kendra had style and taste. I got out the car and went over to her side to open the door for her so I could walk her to her front door. As I stood there waiting for her to get out of the car, she grabbed my shirt and pulled me towards her for a wet kiss. Her tongue tasted sweet and her lips were soft. I almost didn't want the kiss to end, but I caught myself and stepped back. "I didn't mean to come on so strong and put you in a compromising position. I appreciate the ride. I'm sorry," she said before heading toward her grand scale of a wooden door to her mini mansion. I had to be a gentleman. I didn't want her neighbors to see such a beautiful sister being disrespected in any way. I walked her to the door and thanked her for the company at dinner. However, after she took one step inside her house, she made one last ditch effort to get me inside. "You sure you don't wanna caress these instead of being by your lonesome in the hotel room?" she said while fondling her exposed perky breasts. I had to get outta dodge fast before my smaller head prevailed over my big head. Her brown nipples and perky breasts were out of this world. I hadn't been able to suck on Marsha's breasts in so long that I forgot what breasts tasted like. I almost wanted to devour

Kendra, but I turned my back and headed to the car before I could be enticed.

On the drive back to the hotel, all I kept thinking about was Kendra's beauty and sensuality. I didn't think that God was fair to make a person so physically beautiful while he could also make another person so atrociously ugly. I know that I shouldn't call anybody ugly, but damn it, I'd be lying if I said that I've never seen some ugly people. God knows how to give, but I some time wonder if he knows how to equally share his blessings. It's a sin for Kendra to be that fine. I could see why no man in his rabid ass mind would be able to resist her. Back in the day, I would have felt like a sucker for passing on that beautiful piece of ass. I was a changed man, and a family man. I valued what I had at home. At least, that's what I wanted to tell myself so I could feel better about the situation.

The first weekend of my tour went pretty smoothly except for the situation with Kendra. The people in south Florida came out and showered me with lots of love and I appreciated them for it. I was just hoping not to trip up when I got back home because Marsha could smell guilt on my breath. She brought out the guilt detector whenever I did something wrong. I wanted things to be normal without upsetting my wife. The best way to keep from getting tripped up was to talk about the situation with my boys. Once I let it out, there was no way that Marsha could force me to fess up.

The Fellas

Though I was an author, I also had to tend to my business as a publisher. After the regional success of Kevin's first novel, he decided to write a sequel because his audience wanted more. Kevin, Rammell and I became unofficial business partners. Rammell ran the day-to-day operations while Kevin hustled his books and brought in a few more authors to the company. Everybody was eating well and our friendship bloomed to higher heights. Those two knuckleheads also became my confidants. They were the people that I could go and talk about anything. The fact that I was married to Kevin's sister brought us even closer.

After the successful launch of my first book, I decided to move my family to Milton, which is a close suburb to Boston. My business operation ran out of an office I rented on Blue Hill Avenue in Mattapan, located not too far from my house. The back rooms I used as a warehouse for the books and the three front rooms served as offices. Kevin, Rammell and I each have an office while the receptionist is seated at the front. My wife hardly makes it there; one of the few times she came to the office it was to help us hire the right assistant/receptionist. She in no way shape or form was going to allow a beautiful, curvaceous and sassy woman to work for us. She wanted to make sure we stayed focus on business. So she hired Kayla, who has been the best person for the job. Kayla stayed on top of many things, including our catalogs, daily phone orders, prison catalog request and other miscellaneous things. However, the office was also a place where I kicked it with the fellas. Whenever the story was about to get juicy, everyone walked into my office and locked the door. Since Kayla kept a radio on tuned in to her favorite station, we knew she couldn't hear our conversations.

I needed to talk to the guys about what happened over the weekend in Miami. Someone needed to hear how I overcame temptation because of my dedication to my family. I was proud of myself. After I plopped down into my leather arm chair behind my desk, I motioned for my boys to roll their chairs closer, so my conversation couldn't be heard by anybody outside the room. "Kev, who's the finest girl you ever smashed?" while he was thinking about his answer, I asked Rammell the same question. The two of them thought long and hard about the finest women that they had ever been with before giving me an answer. Kevin went with this girl named Millicent who we all agreed was very fine in every aspect of the word. And Rammell chose Roxanne who was neck and neck with Millicent. We all knew each other's women and we didn't mind giving the thumbs up when it was necessary, but there were some mud ducks that we slept with as well. Anyway, I decided to tell the guys to multiply the beauty of their finest women by ten in order to set up the barometer for Kendra's beauty. "Yo, Halle Berry couldn't even stand next to this chick, she was so fine," I told them. "Get the fuck outta here. Ain't no woman finer than Halle Berry," Rammell said. "Man, fuck Halle Berry, Nia Long is the finest chick in Hollywood," Kevin insisted while we nodded our heads in agreement. "How about Sanaah Lathan and Gabrielle Union?" I mentioned. Both Kevin and Rammell shook their heads in agreement with me. "Well guess what, fellas? This chick was finer than all these broads put together. None of them could even carry her jockstrap," I told them in a cocky way. "Word?" Kevin wondered. "That's my word, bruh," I said with confidence. The guys were still waiting for the point of the story. Both of them knew that I couldn't gloat that much about a woman who wasn't mine, so she had to be that fine for me to be talking about her.

"So where you met this chick at?" Kevin asked. "Yo, I met her while I was in Miami this past weekend doing some book signings. Honey was the bomb in every way and she was kicking it hard to your boy," I said while pointing to my chest. Though Kevin and I were cool, I never expected Rammell to ask his dumb-ass question in front of Kevin. "Did you smash?" he asked, looking all stupid in front of Kevin like I was gonna say yes, even if anything happened. "Are you stupid or what? I'm a married man. She was definitely throwing it at a brother, but I passed on it," I said trying not to sound too disappointed in front of Kevin. After explaining the whole situation to them, Kevin wondered if she had ever read his book. Unfortunately, due to our limited distribution, Kevin's books hadn't made it to the stores in Miami yet. But we were working on getting a distribution account with Ingram and Baker and Taylor so that our books could reach more people. We were tired of the black distributors not paying us on time for our books and robbing us altogether. The only honest black distributor we found was African World Books in Maryland. While my story was amusing to the fellas, Kevin and Rammell had their own stories to tell. The two of them always traveled together. Since I started the publishing company and got married, Rammell and Kevin grew closer.

"Man, that's why I don't mind going on the road to promote my book; the honeys always come through to show love. I enjoy the support that I get from the fellas because I represent for my dawgs in everything that I do, but the honeys, oh the honeys can't get enough of them," Kevin bragged. "Yeah, you're right about that," Rammell said while dapping Kevin.

"Yo, I remember this fine ass honey I met in Philly. I was at my man Hak's store doing a signing on a Friday afternoon. It was customary for Hakim to give food to his customers at his store, Black N Nobel, on Fridays, and the place was packed with customers trying to buy the hottest books. I was sitting at the table with my pen in hand and a pack of books neatly stacked when she walked in. Shawty was fine as hell and all eyes were on her. Her booty was like *pow!* and titties just asking a brother to suck on them. Before I said anything to her, I asked my man Tyson and Hak what was up with her, because it was their hood and they seemed very familiar with their customers. After confirming she was one of their regular customers who came in every Friday to get a book, I felt a little more at ease to approach her. I asked shawty if she wanted to check out my book, and the next thing I know we were at the

Marriott crushing," Kevin told us. "What happened?" I asked with curiosity. "Hold up, I know you ain't talking about the shawty who came in with the long weave, knee high boots, black sweater, black leather jacket, blue jeans and the phat booty, are you?" Rammell chimed in. "I see you remember her well," Kevin said. "How could I forget? That was the only time I ever wished I was you," Rammell said enviously.

"Yo, anyway, when I tell you this chick was fine, she was fine and a motherfucking hoodrat. I tore that ass up like I was running from the cops in the projects," Kevin boasted. "I could've told you she was a hoodrat, but she was fine as hell," Rammell confirmed once more. "Man, first of all, we had to stop at the liquor store to get a twelve pack and then this chick had me riding around Philly looking for weed. You know I had my hand on the heater in case she was trying set my ass up. Rammell was in the car looking scared as hell as this chick took us through the worst hoods in west Philly. All I was thinking about was hitting them drawers," Kevin said with a smile on his face. "Yo, shawty had me shaken for a minute cause the weed spots she was taking us to was full of grimy ass looking dudes with gold fronts and mean mugs. I wasn't trying to be a victim, but I knew Kev was holding," Rammell said with comfort. "The fucked up thing, though, was shawty didn't have any friends with her. I had to go to my room to watch ESPN and chill while this dude smashed," Rammell said with disappointment in his voice.

"Yo, can I finish my story?" Kevin asked impatiently. "Go ahead, man. I done heard how you tore her ass up all night that night anyway. Go ahead, man, get your bragging rights," Rammell said sounding annoyed having to hear the story once more. "You know ain't no smoking at the Marriott, so me and shawty had to stay in the car to smoke this Philly blunt, right? By the time we got upstairs, we were high and shit and all we wanted to do was fuck. I popped open a bottle of Heineken and shawty almost guzzled the shit in one gulp, hoodrat style. I was like 'damn!' Word is bond, yo. I was standing in the middle of the room when shawty reached down and pulled my dick out my pants and started sucking on my shit," Kevin revealed. "I ain't that frontin'-ass chick who be talking about I don't suck dick. I love sucking a big dick," shawty said to me. "Yo, do your thing, ma," I told her. Yo, shawty pulled my dick out and was like whoa! I said, you like? She shook her head yes and got on her knees and started slobbing on my shit. Yo, I was standing there wearing my Tims, with my jeans down to my ankles while shawty gave me the blowjob of a lifetime," Kevin was enthused about the story.

"Yo, I almost bust in her face, but I didn't want shawty to think that a brother could bust so quickly and easily, so I held back. I pulled her pants down halfway and turned her around to lean against the bed, put on a condom and started pounding that pussy. Man, that ass was beautiful and I was all up in there. While I was fucking her, she started shaking her ass like a stripper and I lost control. I bust sooner than I wanted and shawty told me she had that effect on men. She didn't know I still had a full tank of gas on reserve. After we took off our clothes, I got on the bed and she straddled me. Man, my shit almost came out of her eye balls, I was so deep in there. She was riding my dick like a bull rider. Her pussy juices started flowing down and I knew I had to tame this chick. I stroked that pussy until her ass collapsed, then we got the motherfucking munchies from smoking all that weed. We ordered room service then went back to fucking for the rest of the night. That was the best hoodrat piece of ass I ever had," Kevin said proudly.

Of course, we had to hear about Rammell's sexcapade as well. The glory couldn't just go to Kevin and me when three men with testosterone were in a room discussing women. No one wants to feel left out, and no man wants his story about a beautiful woman unheard. A good piece of ass is really not that good until your boys hear about it and we were all ears, as Rammell embarked on his journey down to Atlanta where he met the sexy Sasha while he was on tour with Kevin. Those two were like road dawgs once Kevin's book came out. All inspiring female writers looked to Rammell for a book deal, while Kevin banged some of his book groupies.

Silence fell over the room as Rammell broke into his story: "Yo, remember, Sasha, the shawty I met while we were in Atlanta?" he said while pointing to Kevin for confirmation. "Are you talking about the brown skin chick with the pretty toes and big booty?" Kevin asked. "I see you remember her well," Rammell said. "I just remembered your black ass left me hanging til midnight that night. We were supposed to go to the Velvet Room to hang out, and your tired ass showed up talking about, 'I'm too tired to hang.' Yeah, I remember," Kevin said with sarcasm in his voice. "Man, anyway, I gotta tell Dave the story cause he ain't heard it yet," Rammell said trying to hush Kevin.

Rammell began, "We were at Nubian books way on the other side of Atlanta at Southlake mall, Kevin was sitting in the front of the store at the table, while I chatted it up with Marcus inside the store. We were just shooting the shit when Sasha walked in with a group of girls. While the rest of her girls stood in the front to check out Kevin's book, she decided to walk around the store to browse through the inventory. She was checking out books like, the *Blood of My Brother* series, the *Evil Side of Money* series, *Flippin' The Game* and a few others. She was casually dressed in a tight pair of jeans, white t-shirt and a pair of sneakers. Marcus and I instantly took notice of her round butt. I tapped Marcus, 'Yo, check that out.' He nodded in agreement. Sasha was brown-skinned with almond-shaped eyes, shoulder-length hair, a button nose and full kissable lips. I wanted to get at her, but I also didn't want to make it seem like I was harassing Marcus's customers. I asked Marcus if I could holler at her and he gave me the ok." It sounded as if Rammell was about to make this a long–ass, drawn-out story for no reason. "Yo, that's why your ass ain't a writer; you're dragging the story for no goddamn reason. Get to the good part already," I told him. "Man, fuck y'all! Y'all took your time telling your bullshit ass stories and I ain't said shit. You're gonna listen to my shit. Maybe you can add my shit to your books and make them better," he joked. "Stick to running my company, because telling stories ain't your forte," I cracked. Kevin and I gave each other dap, leaving Rammell left out of the writers' circle.

"Again, fuck both of y'all," Rammell said with a light attitude. "Yo, hurry the fuck up and finish the story. Tell homie how you smashed so we can get the fuck outta here. I got a shawty waiting on me," Kevin said impatiently. Rammell cut a look at Kevin that could melt ice. "Anyway, like I was saying...I invited shawty out to dinner and we ended up at the strip club afterwards. When I first met her, I had no idea she was a freak. She looked as conservative as could be. I started telling her how I ran Stories R Us Publications, that's right, I told her I ran it," he emphasized so that I know not to ever call him out on that lie in public. Rammell was the brain behind the growth of the publication company and I always gave him the credit for it. "Man, go on with your story," I said laughing at him. "Shawty aspired to write an erotic book, so she wanted to show me how freaky she could really get. To be honest, I'm tired of all these chicks thinking they can write erotica just because they've sucked and fucked a few dicks. They don't realize it takes writing skills to make it nice and sexy to the readers," Rammell revealed with a bit of frustration. "Oh, now you wanna give us credit for what we do," Kevin said sarcastically. "Man, I know y'all got skills. I would never take that away from y'all. I ain't saying that shit just cause y'all my boys and I work for your black asses. However, you gotta understand my frustration. Y'all don't have to read these tired-ass submissions that I get from these wanna-be writers." You figure if someone wants to be a writer, he would at least try to grasp the basics of grammar before submitting his work to a publishing company, right? But nooo! These motherfuckers want to send me shit that makes no sense, and they want me to publish them," Rammell was obviously frustrated, so he decided to reveal that he fucked the hell out of Sasha and his black ass fell asleep afterwards and didn't wake up til 11:00PM that night to call Kevin. To be honest, his story telling was getting on my nerves. He was all over the fucking place with it.

It was getting late and we barely discussed any business while we were in my office. I decided to call it a day. We walked out to see Kayla on the phone taking an order. It was almost five o'clock and I knew that my wife was waiting on me so she could take a breather from the kids. I rushed up Blue Hill Ave to Milton back to my family.

Can We talk?

From the very beginning of our relationship, I told my wife it was important that we keep an open line of communication. It was customary for me to walk inside my house to find dinner on the table. Whenever I was home, Marsha made sure I ate dinner with the family; that was our time together. After filling up my belly with some of my favorite food, I started to stare into the distance as my wife got up to clear the table. I know to her, it seemed like I was staring at her round booty and imagining how I wanted to take her on the table, but my mind was far from that. I was actually thinking about Kendra and how I almost messed up my marriage. I was hoping not to ever run into her again. Being back at home helped me realized how much my family meant to me and how they depended on me as the head of the household to provide security and stability.

"Babe, when you get a minute, can I talk to you?" I said to my wife with a little bit of angst in my voice. "Let me clear the table and wash the dishes and then I'm all yours," she responded. "How about you just clear the table and I'll wash the dishes later? I want you right now," I said to her in a seductive way. She flashed her beautiful smile that constantly melted my heart. I couldn't believe how fine my woman had become after giving birth to three children. I was in love with her more than ever. As she made her way to the couch to join me, Savant started running around the house with Daniella. My wife had that look on her face as if she wanted to intervene, but I stopped her dead in her tracks when I said, "Just leave them be. I need to talk to my wife for a few minutes. I have things on my mind that I need to share with you." Suddenly, my wife had a concerned look on her face. "Is something wrong, baby?" she asked. "No, there's nothing wrong…at least not yet," I assured her. "What is it that you'd like to talk about then?" she asked with anticipation. "Baby, I don't want this to become a recurring theme in our conversation, but I need to have you so that I don't explode. I can't be going out on tour and salivating over other women because I'm not getting any action from my wife," I mis-communicated. "What! You're cheating on me?" she asked with agitation in her voice. "I think that came out wrong. I meant to say that, because I can't have you, I seem to be looking at other women when I'm on the road. I don't want them or nothing, but they make me think about you," I still wasn't expressing myself correctly.

I figured it was best to stick to writing my thoughts out on paper. I guess that's why I'm a writer and not a speaker. "Are you telling me that you're fantasizing about me while looking at other women? What am I, chopped liver?" she said while impatiently waiting for an answer. "Baby, you got my tongue all twisted up and I don't even know how to express myself. What I really wanna say is that I want some ass and I need some ass soon…from you or I'm gonna explode!" I said while tilting my head to look at the ceiling. "That's all it's about with you, huh? You just wanna have sex with me like I'm some slave who can be turned on at a moment's notice. I don't see you staying home to take care of three kids everyday," she said with obvious anger in her voice. Before the conversation became personal and turned sour, I decided to hand my wife a gift certificate to the spa I had gotten for her to use while I watched the kids. "Baby, I'm sorry. It's just that I've been overwhelmed with the kids and I've needed a break," she said through sobs, as she took the gift certificate from my hand. My wife was grateful that she was getting a day to pamper herself. I was happy to see the relief on her face. I hugged and kissed her and promised to make sure I help more with the children.

There was no need to burden my wife further with my personal desires. I knew that I needed to wait for the right moment to properly discuss my lack of satisfaction in the bedroom. It wasn't even so much a lack of satisfaction, but a lack of ass period. Even my hands were starting to complain. I thought they were gonna file a restraining order against my dick for abuse, I jerked off so much.

Me And The Kids

I have to be honest; I had never had the kids to myself entirely since they were born. I wanted to proceed with caution before I questioned Marsha's complaints and inability to take a breather because of the kids. We started the day very early. My son was the first one up as he gave a damn less whether daddy was in the sweetest stage of sleep where I didn't even want to wake up for any reason at all. But as promised, I told my wife that I would take over all of her duties for the day and I didn't want to renege on my offer. Marsha attempted to get up when she heard Joseph's cries, but I stopped her. "I got this," I said to her as I left the bedroom to check on him. That boy was on his stomach and anxiously waiting for someone to put a bottle in his mouth. I took him out of the crib and held him over my left shoulder while I got his bottle ready. As I waited for it to get warm, I decided to change his wet diaper. I had to be careful because Joseph is a jokester and it almost seemed as if he knew how to time his jokes so he could hit me exactly in the face with his pee. I stepped to the side as I carefully changed him into a new diaper without any incident.

I always enjoyed feeding my son because he has such a voracious appetite. This boy could swallow a bottle whole in less then ten minutes. It was no different this time around. Before I knew it, the other two were up and now I had the full responsibility of my kids. Savant is always the boss of everybody, so whatever she wants to do, she does. This particular morning, Nickelodeon was the order and Dora saved the day. While she watched Dora, I had to carry Daniella into the kitchen to warm up some cream of wheat for them. It was a balancing act I had not yet experienced and I wanted to act like I mastered it while my wife was still in the house. I already knew that it was going to be a long day and the only thing I could pray for was nap time. I sat Daniella in her high chair while I fed her and I encouraged Savant to feed herself. That all worked for about five minutes before she started spreading the cream of wheat all over her face and the couch. That was definitely a scene I didn't want my wife to be privy to. I couldn't compromise my strong stance that it was nothing to take care of three children. I had to clean up before my wife woke up.

Just when I thought it was over after I fed them, my wife walked in the living room and asked, "Did you bathe them yet?" Bathe them? I didn't know they had to take a bath so early in the morning. I was hoping to chill for a few minutes while I allowed them to run around the house. I guessed there was no break for real. And it was just the beginning of the day. I saw the potential for things to get out of hand. I had to quickly think of a way to save face, so I decided the best way to deal with the situation was to take the children out of the house where I could minimize the damage. So I made plans to take them to the Franklin Park Zoo.

My wife could see the challenge ahead, so she reluctantly left the house with no confidence in me whatsoever. I couldn't blame her because I really had no idea how I was going to get through the day without her help. I cautioned her not to call me every minute because I could handle the kids. It didn't necessarily mean that I would call her. I knew the hourly nag would begin the minute she left the house. It was her motherly instincts to protect her children from someone she saw as potentially lacking as a caretaker. I understood.

I'll admit it took me a couple of hours to get the kids ready, but I did it. I washed up very quickly while Savant was glued to the television, Daniella was sitting in her high chair and Joseph was in his play pen. They were all in the living room together. I kept screaming from the bathroom,

"Daddy will be right out." I wanted to make sure that I was present. After I finished getting dressed and got all the necessary essential items that I needed for the day to feed, change and clean the kids, Joseph decided it was the best time to use the bathroom just before we stepped out. It was one of those stinky dumps too. Right after I changed him, Savant needed to use the bathroom as well. So I decided to just check Daniella, too, since they were on a roll.

We finally made it out of the house by noon. I had to make sure Savant was set in her booster seat while Daniella and Joseph had to be seated in their car seats. I almost forgot the double stroller, but my wife made sure that I didn't because she placed it in my way, right in the middle of the garage. She somehow knew that I would forget. All three kids were in the back and I was ready to go. I went over my check list to make sure that I had everything that I needed. And just as I put the car in reverse, my wife called and I heard my phone ringing inside the house. I left my cell phone on the kitchen counter. I ran to the phone and assured my wife that everything was okay. It was just too many damn things to remember, but the cell phone was the most important. Again, thanks to my wife, I was able to leave the house with my phone.

I figured a day at the zoo with my kids would be a cake walk, but boy was I wrong. Maybe my kids were just waiting to let me have it or God wanted me to show more appreciation to my wife for all the work that she had been doing, but these children were hard to manage that day. First of all, Joseph vomited all over himself and I had to change his clothes again. Daniella kept crying for no reason at all and Savant wanted to play with every animal she saw. It was total chaos and I just had to get them back in the car less than a half hour later and head back home. I was at the point where I wanted to call my wife to get some relief, but I didn't. My mom once said that the best way to get the kids to nap is to tire them out, but it wasn't my lucky day. Savant and Daniella had more energy than the Energizer Bunny when we got back home and Joseph only felt comfortable in my arms and would not sit in his chair. Imagine playing with two kids while holding one up in your arm? Not easy. Instead of them getting tired, I was starting to feel a little sleepy. What kind of responsible father falls asleep while watching his kids? It sure as hell wasn't me. So I guzzled down a Red Bull to stay amped up for the kids. I had more energy than ever and was ready to tackle the task of fatherhood. I fed everybody and I told them to bring it on. A few minutes later, every single one of them decided to crash at the same time and now black ass couldn't take a nap because of the Red Bull. I decided to take advantage of my high energy and started working on my next novel while the kids napped.

God must've figured I was punished long enough, because the kids didn't wake up until hours later after my wife and I got a chance to get to know each other's bodies again. It gave me a chance to clean the house, write a few chapters and even cook dinner for my wife. In her eyes, it seemed like I conquered the situation. However, I knew the real deal and I developed a new kind of respect for my wife and her dedication to the family.

Give Me That Body

That look of hunger on my face never disappeared. My wife could see it the moment she walked through the doors. She had just been to the hair salon and the spa, so my baby was looking right. I didn't even get a chance to check out her painted on jeans, halter top and open toe sandals when she left the house that morning, but I took notice of every inch of her body when she returned. Mr. Red Bull was effective as my strain of energy continued to eek from my body. "You look amazing," I said to my wife when she entered the house. She messed me all up when she bit her bottom lip because I knew it was confirmation that I was about to get some ass. I hadn't gotten any booty in so long, my expectations were low. I didn't even know what to do. I think I stripped down in the middle of the living room in a matter of seconds. "Did you forget we have some children in there?" my wife reminded me as she took my hand and led me to the bedroom. In my head, I'm rapping Fat Man Scoop's line "Who's fucking tonight! Who's fucking tonight!" The only thing was, I didn't want to fuck my wife. I wanted to make love to her.

I could tell she wanted to slow down my voracity so she could take care of me like a good wife should. "Baby, I know it's been a while since we've been intimate, but I want you to take your time and make love to me the way you did on our wedding night," she requested. I had no idea I was the man on our wedding night. I always thought that my wife was satisfied 100% of the time whenever we had sex, but she was able to make a distinction between the types of sex we had. It was the first time I realized that. I wanted to take my time with her the way I did that night, but I was afraid that my kids would come and ruin it for me. I didn't want them to wake up in the middle of my nut. Savant was especially bad because she would walk into our room like she owned it. And I know my wife would ignore my ass if she heard one of her babies behind our locked door. It was best for me to go for mine first, I thought.

I wanted to go for mine so badly, but the glare in my wife's eyes told me differently. She was still fully clothed as I stood there butt naked anticipating an explosive sexual attack of her body. Instead, I pulled her toward me and started kissing her ever so gently. It had been so long since we shared an intimate moment, I almost didn't want to let her lips go. Her lips were always soft and tasty to me. I savored them as if it were the first time we were kissing. Feeling my wife's curvaceous body in my arms was the best thing that happened in our household since we brought my children home from the hospital. I wanted to feel her warmth and presence. She held on to me tight as tears streamed down her beautiful face because she knew that I missed her and I could feel that she missed me too. We stood there in a long embrace as my naked body rested on her fully-clothed one. We didn't have to speak any words. The gaze into each other's eyes said enough for us to understand that we needed to bring the intimacy back into our lives.

Still, I could not let this opportunity pass me by. I needed to have sex with my wife. I glided my hand down to her pants as she raised her arm to pull off her halter top. I could not believe that this woman had just given birth to my son a couple of months ago. Her body was more desirable than ever. She was blessed with good genes, and after three kids, she still had no stretch marks or overly -extended belly. I'm sure I would have loved her the same regardless. She must've had a Brazilian wax while at the spa because her pubic hair was shaped in a little heart right above her clitoris. While I fondled my way around her goodies, she whispered in my ear, "Take me, baby. Make love to me again." As if my Johnson wasn't already hard enough, I swear I could feel more blood flow after her whisper. I slowly placed small kisses all over her body while my fingers caressed her nipples. I wish I could've sucked on her nipples, but I knew her milk wouldn't do my body good, so I left it for my son. However, I made my way down to her milky domain below because I longed to taste her nectar. We were standing in the middle of the room and my wife held on to my head as my tongue made contact to her clitoris. "Mmmh, baby," she whispered, confirming that my skills hadn't diminished. She tasted so good. I didn't even want to come up for air. I parted her lips and stuck my tongue inside of her wetness lightly. She couldn't stand it any longer. She motioned me toward the bed where she sat up on the edge while I continued my oral safari of her African terrain.

In and out my tongue stroked my wife, forcing her to grind on my face while holding on to the bed sheets as ecstasy exited her body. She shook and cried like a woman who had been deprived. The sensible touch of my hands on my wife's body made her shiver. I knew it was time to make her feel like a woman. She moved up on the bed as I climbed on top of her to allow her the full extent of my love. I slid right in and it fit perfectly like it always did. The slippery wetness of her vagina consumed my penis and it felt like heaven. Our breath met in the middle of my third stroke and I held on to her tongue in my mouth as I continued to make love to her. The sexual reconnection was heavenly and I was grateful, happy, content and appreciative of her generosity. As much as I wanted us to make love for the rest of the night, I knew that my daughter would soon wake up from her nap. As my wife straddled to work on her third orgasm, I decided to let go and have one of my own. I held on to her thighs as she grinded on me while we both came in unison. A brief moment after she collapsed in my arms, we heard little footsteps coming from my daughter's room. It our cue to get up and put on something decent so we could revert back to our roles as parents. I just hoped that my wife could be as generous again sooner rather than later.

On The Road Again

Despite the fact that it was difficult to leave my family on the weekend, I had to do what I had to do. My book had to be promoted and the success it relied solely on me. I was the publisher, writer, marketing person and everything else associated with that particular book. Not to mention, I also had employees as well as my family depending on the success of my publishing company. Hitting the road was nonnegotiable. As usual, I packed my bags earlier the previous evening, played with my kids and went to bed with my wife by my side. I knew she left in the middle of the night because she had to keep waking up to feed Joseph and change his diaper. She stayed in Savant's room in order for me to get some rest. My wife was very considerate when it came to my rest. I never said goodbye to my family when I left them because I knew that I would be back soon enough. I made it a point to kiss each and everyone of my children and my wife and always told them I would see them later. That was my assurance to my family whenever I left for the road.

It has always been easier for me to travel early because there's seldom any delay with the earlier flights. Needless to say, I was at the airport by 5:00AM to catch my 6:00AM flight from Boston to Atlanta. The usual herd of business men trying to make it back home to their families crowded the airport. Since I like to use my time efficiently, I always make it a priority to print out my boarding pass from home because I don't like to wait until I get to the airport to do it. The line through security was out the door and it was just my luck that this little old lady in front of me was wearing any kind of metal shit she could find in her closet that morning. She had to walk through the metal detector at least five times before she was finally cleared to go through. I was standing there impatiently waiting and hoping that I would not miss my flight. I only had a half hour to board and my gate was the farthest of all of them. That's one of the disadvantages of carry-on baggage. It's difficult to run through the airport hauling a suitcase and a shoulder bag with a computer through the airport. Though I was in shape, I was sweating like an inmate standing before a firing squad. By the time I reached the gate, they had called my name three times over the PA system. Luckily, I made my flight and was on my way to Atlanta with enthusiasm for a great weekend.

I would normally look over a manuscript while I'm on a long flight, but this particular morning I just wanted to close my eyes and get a little more sleep. There was a huge difference between what I had hoped to do and what I ended up actually doing. Again, it was just my luck that I sat next to the guy with the foulest breath on a full flight, and he wanted to have a conversation. At first, I tried to form this frowning disinterested look on my face so he wouldn't talk to me, but it didn't work. "Where are you headed?" he asked after I sat down in the aisle seat. The funk from his breath almost burned the hair in my nose. I was thinking to myself, *there's no fucking way in the world that this man didn't smell his shitty breath before he left his house.* And since he was wearing a wedding band, I assumed his wife had to have been victim of that breath before he got me, and she should've said something so that I would not have become a casualty of his halitosis. Shitty was really an understatement for this guy's breath. His breath smelled like he had been eating ass that just got up from a toilet. Some people are kinky like that and have these weird fetishes, so you never know! He was definitely a talker. I found out he was from Boston and was on his way to Atlanta to do some work at the corporate headquarters for Home Depot. The very first time I decided to fly first class in my life ended up being the worst experience of my life. I would have switched seats with someone in coach just so I could breathe easier away from this man. I even put on my sunglasses to signal to him that I wanted to rest and for him to keep his doo-doo breath on lock.

The weird thing about the situation was that the man was kind and genuine. I couldn't be rude to him. He wanted to know what I did for a living and asked questions about my family. It was one of those "white people situations" of small talk. I got the feeling that everyone in first class could smell his breath and they could feel my pain. Even the waitress who was serving drinks in first class stayed away from our row. His bad breath was confirmed by the rest of the passengers when he got up to use the bathroom and everyone put their hand over their nose to signal that they could smell his breath. One guy even told me he felt sorry for me having to sit next to the obese man with the bad breath. Nevertheless, I never got my sleep and I was happy when the flight finally landed.

Relieved that I was away from sewer breath, I ran off of the plane before he could get a chance to carry on with his conversation again. I made it down to the train and the baggage claim terminal in no time. I went over and caught another shuttle train to Hertz to pick up my rental car. After picking up a Mazda 6, I called the Marriot in Smyrna to see if they would allow me to check in early. They agreed to accommodate me and I was able to get a couple of hours of rest before I went to my first signing at Borders on Peachtree Rd in Brookwood Place near Buckhead.

Guess Who's Back?

I've always considered myself to be a forward-thinking man, so I decided to use the social networking sites to allow my readers to know my whereabouts so they could attend my book signings. I've always had two Facebook pages - one personal and the other for my company. The company one is where I usually post my activities and it's also where everyone is welcomed as a friend. At the company, we assume everyone who sent friend requests to us is interested in our books. We never turned down a friend request unless it was some extreme crap. Unbeknownst to me, I was giving a stalker access to me.

I showed up at my signing a little late. Well, fifteen minutes late to be exact. I never understood why there was always traffic in Atlanta. Where in the world are people going at twelve o'clock in the afternoon? Anyway, I apologized to the manager at Borders for my tardiness before I took my seat behind the table to start signing my books. It was a typical signing other than the fact that Kendra from Miami showed up in Atlanta. I was a little alarmed by her presence. She had already bought my books twenty-five times over and she claimed she read the previous one. What was her purpose there? "How are you? You seem a little surprised to see me," she said after approaching my table. Shit, I was praying this chick wasn't carrying a gun or some kind of vendetta because of my story. "I'm fine," I said with hesitation in my voice. "How've you been?" I asked reluctantly, hoping not to engage her further in a conversation. "I'm well. I was hoping to hear from you after our dinner," she said. "I did tell you that I was married, right?" I asked with a perplexed look on my face. "Yeah, you told me. You can't have any friends because you're married?" she asked. "I suppose I can, but I'm very picky when it comes to friendships. And it takes a lot for me to allow someone into my space," I told her. "Is that right?" she asked with obvious disapproval in her voice. "Well you know how people can be sometimes. I'm just careful. I don't want to open myself up to some lunatic and end up paying the price for it," I said to her without looking up at her. "I know you're busy right now with your signing, how about we meet up for drinks at Justin's later?" she suggested. "I really would like that, but I can't. I have another signing at Borders in the Stonecrest Mall at 4:00PM. I have to take a rain check on that offer," I told her. "Ok. I guess I'll catch up with you then," she said before making her exit out the door.

The book signing went well enough. I was happy with the amount of readers who came to show their support. After my signing, I decided to go to Houston's for a quick bite to eat because my stomach was screaming with hunger. I had a tall glass of lemonade to wash down my gourmet burger and fries. After re-energizing myself, it was time to head out to Lithonia for my next signing at the Stonecrest Mall. I only had one hour to reach my destination in Lithonia and again, I had to maneuver my way through Atlanta's never-ending traffic. While on my way to the bookstore, I called my wife to check on her and the kids. Everything was great and I was feeling fine. I reached my destination just in time. The store manager, Jeremiah, was there to greet me. After setting me up with a table by the entrance of the store, he brought my books and the hustle began all over again. One by one the books started flying off my table as each customer who entered the store had to cross my path in order to get to the other side. Intrigued by the racy nature of my book covers, they stopped to ask questions. After breaking down the synopsis of each, more often than not, it ended up in a sale. This particular aspect of my job had become routine and I had my pitch down to a science. My books were also often sold the minute a reader decided to randomly browse through the pages.

It was almost 6:00PM and my signing was about to end, when I looked up, I again saw Kendra standing before me with a big smile on her face. I realized the mistake I made earlier when I told her that I would be at Borders until 6:00PM for my next signing back in Buckhead. "I hope you're not going to turn down my offer for a drink this time. We can go to Barnacles across the mall," she suggested. I felt cornered by her and I didn't know how to get out of it, so I reluctantly agreed to join her for a drink. I must not have been paying attention because I was still high from the loving I received from my wife the day before, but all eyes seemed to have been on Kendra as she strutted her stuff through Borders. Her wrap-around dress fit comfortably around her sexy body and her calves just spoke of her work ethics in the gym. She had some beautiful strong legs and a strut to die for. Still, I hadn't taken noticed that day until all the men started gawking over her.

She led the way to the exit as I followed behind her and I couldn't help noticing her essence. As much as I wanted to ignore Kendra, I realized that I was still a man and my senses were sensitive to the sight of a beautiful woman. We started to converse while walking to Barnacles.

I decided to leave my car in the Borders parking lot because she pointed Barnacles to me across the way. Besides, an easy stroll never hurts the body. I couldn't quite make out the name of the perfume that Kendra was wearing and I damn sure wasn't going to ask her. I suspect it was Juicy Couture because my wife sometimes wore the same perfume, and it was my favorite. "How long are you in Atlanta?" she asked with curiosity. I didn't want to be too definite, so I decided to give her a vague answer, "I'm not sure. I might leave after my signing tomorrow. I didn't necessarily lie to her, but I damn sure didn't want her to know that I was leaving Sunday evening. "What about you, what are you doing in Atlanta?" I asked. "Well, I came to see an old friend that I hadn't seen in a while," she said. I didn't yet want to make the correlation or distinction between fan and stalker, as it related to Kendra, but I was on the fence.

We walked into Barnacles and it was as if Moses parted the sea. Everybody stood on the side to take a glimpse of the beautiful woman walking beside me. I felt a little uncomfortable because she drew so much attention. I felt like I was cheating on my wife and I tried as much as I could to create plenty of space between us. I didn't want anybody in that to think that she was my woman. The last thing I needed was for someone to call my wife or write on the internet that they saw another woman on my arm. Under the circumstances, I wouldn't be surprised if something like that got back to my wife. I also couldn't blame my wife if there was any lack of trust based on the way that we met and my history. I was a dick slinger when we met.

After taking a seat at the bar on a couple of stools, I ordered a Corona while she ordered a Screaming Orgasm. She was starting to drop too many hints for me, I became guarded. "A Screaming Orgasm, huh?" I asked. "That's just the way I like 'em. I got to scream when I have one," she revealed while licking her lips and looking at me. At any other time, the bulge in my pants would have wiped that flirtatious grin off her face, but I was focused. I had Marsha on my mind and my three children. I clinked my bottle with her glass to cheer our reconnection, if you will. There was music playing and the tiny dance floor was packed with people. I got up from my stool to look at the crowd while holding my beer in my hand. It looked like the mature crowd was having the best of time. Most of the brothers looked like they just came from work, representing in their Armani suits, a few off the rack suits and some suits that shouldn't be called suits because they were so bright and poorly designed. I was wearing my favorite Guess jeans, a button down baby blue and white shirt and a light blue blazer with a pair of brown shoes. It was a little casual compared to most people in the crowd, but I was comfortable.

As I started to bob my head to the beat, I set my beer on the counter so I could clap, as instructed by the DJ. "Clap, clap, clap your hands," the voice blared over the speaker. I didn't even realize I was so much into the music. "I see you don't mind getting your groove on," Kendra commented. "I can get down," I said confidently. I wasn't so much a dancer as I was a two-stepper. "You wanna hit the floor?" she asked. I figured why not. I took a long swig of my beer before heading to the dance-floor with Kendra in tow. I can't recall exactly but I think "Atomic Dog" was the song that called everyone to the floor, including every Q-Dog in the house. They can't let their anthem play without acting a fool to it. Kendra proceeded to get a little freaky with me on the dance-floor by strategically placing her ass against my pelvis while she backed into it. I can't lie, her backside looked pretty good and I almost developed a boner, which is natural for a man to do. We danced to a few more songs before returning to the bar to order another drink.

I couldn't even tell you when the room went black. All I knew was that I woke up in Kendra's bed in my boxers while she was in the kitchen making breakfast. "What happened? How did we end up back here? I thought you lived in Florida?" I asked her furiously. "I don't know, Lover Boy, you tell me how we ended up here? I forgot to tell you that I also have a home here in Georgia," she responded sarcastically. "You're fucking kidding me, right?" I asked cautiously. "You didn't mind being in here last night when you were fucking the hell outta me," she revealed to me. "What the hell are you talking about? I didn't fuck you!" I said with anger. "Maybe a little proof might do it for you," Kendra said as she pressed play on the DVD player so I could watch my performance the previous night. I hardly performed, but the picture was perfectly clear as Kendra pulled off my underwear while I lay on her bed. My dick was hard as hell as she sucked the skin off it. She even rode me for a good fifteen minutes. I didn't quite see the expression on my face, but I could easily tell it was me. My only problem was that I didn't remember any of it. *How could I have fucked a woman in a state of sub-consciousness?* I asked myself. "Where the hell are my clothes?" I demanded. "Your clothes are in the closet in the master bedroom," she said with a sarcastic smile on her face. "I'm gonna get dressed and get the hell outta here. Something's wrong with you. And I'm taking this DVD with me, too," I said as I pulled the DVD out.

After running back upstairs to get dressed, Kendra stormed into the room and started ranting, "Where the hell do you think you're going, back to your little wife and kids like nothing happened between us? You think you're just gonna fuck me and leave me?" She said with a crazed look in her eyes. I didn't know what the fuck was wrong with her, but I was ready to knock her right the fuck out if she tried anything funny. I quickly got dressed and made my way out the door. After stepping out the door, I realized my rental was nowhere to be found. "Where the hell is my car?" I asked in a sadistic tone. "Since you didn't feel like driving last night, we left your car in the parking lot and you rode with me," Kendra said with a smirk on her face. "Well, I need you to take me back to my car," I said, confused. Kendra just smiled at my request. "Now!" I screamed with anger. "You better slow your roll and watch your tone in my house before my neighbors call the cops out here. I could press charges and tell them that you raped me, but I won't because I like you and I think you like me, too," she said, delusional. "Are you out of your fucking mind? You must have a fucking screw loose or something. I have a family, a wife and three kids. I don't fucking like you. You know what? I'm gonna catch a cab back to my car," I said as I headed back out the door. I took a few steps forward while rummaging through my pockets for my cell phone, but I couldn't find it. I walked back to her house and just as I was about to ring the bell to the palatial home, which I took notice of, finally, she opened the door and said, "You're looking for this?" she handed me my phone with an even bigger smirk on her face. I swear I wanted to knock her ass out.

As I walked out the subdivision towards the street, I had no idea what part of town I was in. I had to stop a man to ask him where I was. He informed me I was in Snellville, Georgia, which was about a fifteen minute drive from the Stonecrest mall. After going through the 411 operator to find a local cab, I decided to wait on Annistown Road to get picked up. It didn't take very long for the cab to show up. After getting in the cab, the driver was trying to make small talk, but I was deep in thought trying to figure out what had just happened to me. It was kind of strange to me that Kendra would have such an immaculate and spacious house in Georgia while she claimed she lived in Florida. I didn't know what I had gotten myself into. I needed to cancel my book signings for the rest of the day so I could regain my sanity. I felt bad about it, but I called Marcus to see if we could reschedule for another time. He wasn't too happy because of the last minute cancellation, but I didn't want to divulge my personal business to him.

Oh What a Night!

I finally made it back to my car, and I was pleasantly surprised that it wasn't towed. I paid my cab fare and was on my way. I went back to my hotel contemplating my next move. I had no idea what happened, but I had planned on watching the rest of the DVD to see what the hell I was doing fucking this woman when I had a wife at home. My mind was racing and heart was beating a mile a minute. It almost felt as if I was losing grip on myself. I was glad I got a hold of the DVD before she decided to do something sinister with it, like getting it to my wife. I was trying my best to recollect the events of the previous night, but I kept drawing a blank. I don't even remember leaving the bar with this chick. I knew my black ass should've turned down her request for a drink, but against my better judgment, I made a poor decision.

First, I wanted to wash her dirty paws off me. I jumped in the shower and washed almost twenty minutes. I scrubbed and scrubbed and scrubbed until I couldn't scrub anymore. The guilt of being with another woman was pulling at my heart and I needed to find my own sanity to deal with it. After stepping out of the shower, I wanted to see what I had done with this woman and why I couldn't remember any of it. I popped the DVD into the disc drive on my laptop and I began to watch what unfolded. I wasn't sure at what point she started to record the session, but I was butt naked on her bed when it came on and she was kneeling between my knees giving me what appeared to be a great blowjob. I held on to the back of her head as she took my dick in and out her mouth. It seemed like I was a willing participant. She must've sucked my dick for a good fifteen minutes before she asked me to lie down on my back while she straddled me.

Straddling me was one thing, but it was alarming to me when I noticed that I was not wearing a condom. Kendra rode me like a stallion and was talking shit the whole time she was doing it. "You ain't never had no pussy like this, huh?" she said as she took all my nine inches inside of her. I held on to her ass and sucked on her breasts while she fucked the hell outta me. "Tell your pretty wife that you found some better pussy, and she better step her game up if she wants this good dick," she said. I couldn't believe my dumb ass replied, "I will tell her." "This is your pussy. You can fuck it any way you want and however you want. Fuck me, baby," she screamed before sticking her tongue in my mouth while fixated on the camera. This went on for about fifteen minutes before I heard, "I'm coming, baby." I couldn't believe it. Then she said, "Yes, come for mama." I knew then that I was in a whole lot of trouble.

I needed to figure out why I couldn't remember any of what happened the previous night. So I decided to jump on the internet to see the symptoms of my condition. While googling different sites, I came across one thing that made more sense than anything else that I found on the internet. I had to have been given a psychedelic substance that erased my memory to force the kind of amnesia where I couldn't recall anything. The question now was, how was it done and when? I needed to figure those things out and I also wanted to know why.

In my heart of hearts, I didn't want to believe that Kendra was a stalker, but the reality was that she was. I wished I had owned up to that reality. My next plan of action was nothing because I didn't know what to do. I was more afraid than anything. At that point, I didn't even want to be in Atlanta anymore. I wanted to just pack my bags and head home. However, if I went home so abruptly, I would raise my wife's suspicions, which was something I didn't want to do.

Melodrama

It was getting a little late in the day and I was getting hungry. I wanted to eat lunch, so I decided to order room service because I didn't have the energy to leave my hotel room. After eating my meal and drinking a glass of wine to help calm my nerves, I decided to turn on the television as a distraction. Unfortunately, "A Thin Line Between Love and Hate," starring Martin Lawrence and Lynn Whitfield was playing on the Movie Channel. It was the worse movie that could've been on at the time. Watching the crazy antics of the character played by Lynn Whitfield forced me to reconsider my situation and think about my position. I wasn't going to let Kendra get the best of me if she was indeed crazy. No way was I going to let this woman ruin my life and my marriage.

I also realized I needed to call Kendra to make sure she understood my stance and I wasn't going to take her bullshit. The only problem was that I didn't have her number. I realized that I never got her number, but no sooner was I thinking about calling her she text me a picture of her performing oral sex on me. I was furious and I just knew that I had to put a stop to her shenanigans. I called her right back with the most irate tone, "What the fuck do you think you're doing? Are you fucking sick in the head or what?" There was a pause on the phone for about thirty seconds before she responded, "Let's see, maybe your wife might be able to explain my craziness when she sees the picture of your dick in my mouth." I almost swallowed my tongue when she mentioned my wife. "You are sick! You better keep my wife and family out of this or we're gonna have problems!" I threatened. "Now your family's important to you. You weren't saying that last night when you were knee deep in my pussy. You know what? I don't even care that you have a wife. I just want to make sure I get a piece of you when I want you," she said in as serious a tone as she could muster. I was thinking to myself that this woman was either schizophrenic or plain old nuts. "I don't know what the hell you think this is, but there ain't gonna be no me and you. I'm thinking that you raped me last night and I might call the cops and file charges on you," I tried to scare some of my logic into her. "It's a good thing that we have a DVD showing that you were a willing participant in what went on last night. Go ahead, take your punk-ass to the police and tell them how you got raped by a woman," she said in an attempt to emasculate me.

This was something new for me. At this point, I was feeling like drama followed me wherever I went. I needed to calm down, pull myself together and come up with a plan to get rid of this woman. "Look I don't know what your agenda is, but I'm sure that we can work something out. Tell me what you want, but I need you to go away after I take care of it," I told her. "Go away? Now why would I want to go away from the man I love? You got this wrong. I don't need anything from you but your heart. That little skank you ended up marrying doesn't deserve you. You just need some time to figure that out. Meanwhile, I'm thinking about sending her a copy of that DVD to show her what a great time we had together," she said in a threatening way. "You better keep my wife out of this. Besides, I have the DVD and I plan on destroying it," I confirmed. "I know you don't think I'm that stupid. You don't want to be with a stupid woman, anyway, and that is why you need to be with a smart sassy woman who made enough copies of that DVD to send to your wife's entire family, including her little thug brother that you fear so much," she revealed.

Apparently, Kendra had been doing her homework and planning the situation all along. She just knew a little too much about my family, or maybe I just revealed too much in that damn book that I wrote. The deck of cards in my hands weren't even good enough to pull a good bluff. Kendra had me cornered and I needed to rethink my position once again as I dealt with her. For the sake of my marriage, I needed to revert back to my old ways so I could get rid of this woman. Killing her was not an option because I was not a killer, but I had to use what I got to get what I wanted and I wanted to get rid of her ass as soon as possible. Kendra was in for a fight and I knew that the battle had just begun. "Look, I understand that you like me, and I like you, too, but we should take our time to make sure this lasts. I'm gonna need to get to know you better so we can take our relationship to the next level," I said to her over the phone while trying my hardest to hold in my laugh. Since she was loony, I needed to be completely deranged as well to deal with her schizophrenic ass. The game was on.

"I knew you liked me, you were just trying to fight it. What's not to like about me? I promise I'm gonna make you the happiest man in the world," her delusional ass told me. "I can already tell that you're all about me, and that's something that every man wants. You're fine as hell, sexy, smart and caring," I told her, trying to soothe her ego. I really wanted to tell her stupid ass how deranged and crazy she was, but I had to play along. I couldn't risk losing my family over something that I didn't purposely do. "When are you leaving town? I would love to spend some more time with you," she suggested. I hadn't noticed up until this point how annoying her baby-sounding voice was. She sounded like she was whining 24/7. "I guess we can meet later to catch a movie or something," I appeased her. "Good. I can pick you up from the hotel around 8:00PM," she confirmed. "I'll see you at 8:00 then," I said before hanging up the phone.

What the hell did I get myself into? After weighing my options, they all led down the same path- to the destruction of my marriage. I knew I couldn't tell Marsha that I agreed to have drinks with this woman because she would automatically believe that I was interested in her; I couldn't go to the police because it would eventually lead back to my wife; I couldn't kill her because I would spend the rest of my life in prison and away from my kids. I felt I was running out of options. Though I agreed to play putty in her hands, I still had to figure out a plan to get rid of this woman. My mind was all over the place and I was stressed out about the possibility of losing my family over this bullshit. Not only that, I didn't know how crazy this chick was. And I did not want her to take this shit to my doorstep.

Game Time

Kendra showed up at my hotel at 8:00PM to pick me up as planned. It was the most provocative that I had ever seen her dress. She had on a black leather mini-skirt that barely covered her thick thighs and black halter top that was so tight, it seemed like her nipples were rubbing against each other through her cleavage. She was wearing bright red high heel pumps, bright red lipstick and she was carrying a red purse. I was already dressed when she got there because I had no plan to invite her into my room. However, I did take inventory of her outfit, and her raunchy sexiness couldn't be denied. But my mind was set on getting rid of her and my dick wouldn't even get hard with an injection shot at that moment. She pulled me in for an embrace and whispered in my ear, "I'm not wearing any panties especially for you tonight." I knew then it was going to be a long night and alcohol was going to play a big role in it.

I never thought a woman so beautiful could become so ugly to me. We decided to go to Justin's for dinner because she wanted to be seen. At first, I objected to going to Justin's because there was a possibility that I could be spotted on the arm of this vixen, but she pleaded and I agreed to go because I wanted her to believe that I was all about her. After having a couple of drinks at the bar while we waited to be seated, I started to relax a little. I figured if I was going to pull this off, I needed an Oscar-caliber performance to make Kendra believe that I was real and true. I swear the whole place came to a halt when Kendra and I walked through the door. It was as if everyone stopped what they were doing to stare at her, showing off bare legs in five-inch heels and a mini skirt. The men couldn't stop taking glances while the women stared in awe and envy. I wanted to play the simpleton role, but the true cocky Dave started to emerge. I held Kendra's hand confidently in mine after loosening up from the alcohol. Not only were the people staring at her, they were also staring at me now. I wore basic black and my outfit was a killer as well. Black flat-front virgin wool pants, a black V-neck cashmere sweater, black Gucci shoes and my silver Movado watch. Of course, I couldn't leave the house without my signature cologne, D&G # 10, La Roue De La Fortune. We looked like a powerful attractive couple and heard whispers of such throughout the room. I guess that was the fantasy Kendra had when she decided to stalk me. Honestly, we did make an attractive couple on the surface, but this lunatic had to go. My wife and I made an even better couple because we had love.

After we were seated at a table by the window overlooking Peachtree Street, Kendra started taking advantage of the dimly lit corner and she began to flirt with me. I could stare into her light brown eyes and see nothing but malice through that beautiful smile. The gliding of her tongue across her wet-looking red lips would have had my dick hitting the bottom surface of the table under normal circumstances, but this situation wasn't normal. I prayed to God that nobody in the restaurant knew my wife or recognized me as a writer. I knew how devastating it would be for my wife to find out I was out with another woman. She had gone through that in her past relationship with her ex-husband. I didn't want her to be victimized twice. I flashed a phony smile toward Kendra with the hope of having her pull that tongue back into her mouth while the whole restaurant stared at us. Suddenly, what she was doing didn't seem sexy at all to me. It seemed gross. I'm sure the gawking men sitting around me were having the time of their lives. I even noticed a few of them getting hit over the head by some real Gucci, Chanel and Louis Vuitton purses, as well as some fake ones, by their women for staring at the woman sitting across from me. I was in the Black fronting capital of the world and everyone at the restaurant that night pulled their best gear out of the closet to be seen. The fact that Kendra pulled up to the valet in a black convertible CLK, Mercedes Benz had the people wondering who they hell we were. It was just a coincidence that our colors matched that night.

Since I had brought my last drink from the bar over to the table, I decided to just gulp it down to free my mind from the bondage sitting before me. I waited for the waitress to come back so I could order another drink, but she was taking her sweet time. I figured it would be easy to avoid having a conversation with Kendra if I acted like I was drinking. Kendra didn't need words to communicate with me, however. As we continued to look at each other while I kept throwing fake smiles at her, she found a way to aggravate me even more. Kendra took off her shoes and proceeded to grope me under the table with her bare foot. Unfortunately, she never got the reaction she sought. My dick didn't budge or bulked up. I was irritated by her and I wished I could reach across the table and slap that silly smile off her face. Though her smile was more on the seductive side to the other admirers who were in the restaurant staring at her, it didn't have the same effect on me. I felt like I was caught in her web of deception and I was trying to find a way out.

The waitress finally came and we decided to order our drinks and food at the same time. I opted for the Sautéed Red Snapper and a Kamikaze on the rocks, and she ordered P. Diddy's Seafood Pan Plate and a Cosmopolitan. The fondling of my penis under the table by her foot continued and the agitation on my face was getting harder to contain. After the continuous pestering of my dick by her big toe for about five minutes, I decided to finally grab hold of her foot hard tight as I politely told her, "I'd rather you not do that right now because it's annoying." She rolled her eyes and said "You don't know how to have any fun," then sucked her teeth. At least I had some good food to look forward to. When my food finally arrived after a short wait, I dove in head first to savor the deliciously cooked red snapper. As I masticated my food, I kept looking up to see what Kendra was doing, and she was staring dead at me. "You're a little hungry today, aren't you?" she asked sarcastically. I just nodded my head to acknowledge her comment, so that I wouldn't have to verbally engage in a conversation with her. I didn't know what expectations Kendra had for after dinner, but my plan was to go back to the hotel to get some rest so I could be out on the first flight the next morning.

I took a peek over to her plate and noticed that it was barely touched. She was eating like a bird and trying her best to seduce me with the movement of her mouth as she chewed her food. Inside, I was laughing harder than a hyena. However, the other drooling men around us seemed to be entertained to the fullest. I wish she could have spotted one of them to take home with her so she could leave me the hell alone, but to no avail. I had never met a woman who was so into me for no reason at all. I needed to know from her the reason she was fascinated with me. "Can I ask you something?" I said to her. She nodded to confirm it was okay. "Out of all the authors out there, why do you like my work so much?" I asked, hoping to get some kind of vague vanity answer. "Well, that's a pretty interesting question. When I was reading your book, *Doggy Style*, I felt as if you were talking about me. I felt the pain of the character and I understood your sympathy for the character. That alone told me that you have a kind heart and you understand love. I felt Sheila was looking for love despite all her success, but she kept getting dogged by most of the men who came into her life," she answered. I was a little shocked that she remembered so much about the book. I guess she was a true fan of my work. "You said you can identify with Sheila, how so?" I asked. "Oh, I can identify with Sheila in many ways. I'm sure I don't have to tell you that I'm successful in my career – I'm a lawyer, by the way - but I keep meeting men who don't appreciate my success or they can't handle it altogether. I was forced to date men in the same tax bracket as me, but those men are not interested in a woman like me. I'm not light enough for them."

Kendra was definitely a light-skinned sister who looked good enough to be a starlet, but I started to wonder if her over-the-top controlling attitude had a lot to do with the failures she experienced in her personal relationships. "What makes you think that the men are to blame for the problems that you've had in the relationships with them?" I asked cautiously. I had to be careful because it was already established that this lady was cuckoo. "I know it's not me. I'm not the one saying 'yeah baby I love you' only to not hear from that person after I've given myself to them. Or they want to change this and that about me after they've fucked me. Most men are full of shit and I seemed to have been meeting all the ones who are filled to the top," she said angrily. "What makes you think that I'm different from the rest of these men?" I asked curiously. "You're a man of honor. You just married the wrong woman. I like the fact that you accepted your responsibility and decided to do right by your wife. That's very honorable in a man," she said, almost in a congratulatory way. "If you know that I'm an honorable man, then why are you even wasting your time pursing this?" I asked anxiously. I couldn't wait to hear her explanation for wanting to take me away from my wife. "That's easy to explain. I believe that we crossed paths for a reason and I read your book for a reason. It was because of your book that I realized there were still some good men out there. And I'm a fighter. So I decided to fight for your love. If your wife really loves you, there's no reason why she shouldn't fight to keep you," she told me astonishingly. This woman was beyond delusional, I thought.

By then, I realized there was no rationality at all to this woman and there was also no need to engage her in a conversation. Before I could get the image of this insane woman ruining my life out of my head, she leaned toward me and said in a low whisper,"Are you ready for dessert? My kitty is calling your name." She started to touch herself seductively and I knew that we had to get out of there before she embarrassed us both. "You're ready to do this?" I asked her, creating the most tense anticipation of buck-wild sex with my tone and eyes. She just knew that I was gonna fuck the hell out of her when we got back to the hotel. And she moved like it too, as she stormed out of the restaurant, not even giving me enough time to pay the bill. We were at the valet in no time picking up the car. Like a gentleman, the valet opened the driver side door for her to get in, while I let myself in the car on the passenger side.

I was so occupied with the way Kendra was zooming in and out of traffic that I didn't realize she was driving to her house instead of dropping me off at The Marriott hotel as planned. It took less than twenty five minutes to make it from Buckhead to Snellville, a ride that would usually take a good forty-five minutes without traffic. After pulling into her garage, Kendra told me she had a special treat for me and all I needed to do was be her audience. "How about you drop me off at the hotel like we talked about?" I said to her. "It's still early. You've got plenty of time to rest for your flight tomorrow. I wanna make sure we have some fun tonight because I don't know when I might see you again. Besides, I'm sure you'd rather have fun with me tonight than have me show up at your house in Boston," she said matter –of-factly. I was really getting sick of her threats, but I also didn't want her to carry it out either. "Guess what? I'm gonna be the best audience you have ever had. So let the show begin!" I said while smiling at her lunatic ass.

I had no idea what I was in for, but I agreed to be part of her audience, well the only audience to her show. Kendra popped a mixed CD in her stereo in the car and left the door open. As she was inserting the CD in the stereo, she started shaking her no-panties-having ass. I could see the crease of her shaven pussy from the back as her short skirt rolled up above her ass. She then turned around and sat on the front of the hood of the car while leaning the rest of her body back and her legs spread apart. While the sound of Usher's "I Wanna Make Love in Da club," blared through the speakers, Kendra commenced her strip tease on the hood of the car. For a moment, I was lost in her performance and was actually enjoying the show. I was never one to be turned on by strippers, so I found Kendra to be quite entertaining. "I never knew a lawyer could have so much hidden talent," I said to her. "There's always more than meets the eye with everybody. Do you like?" she asked while biting her bottom lip and sensually running her hands up her inner thighs attempting to entice me. I was entertained, but not enticed. My goal was to save my marriage. And I would do almost anything to do it.

Kendra continued to move to the sound of the beat and little by little she started shedding her clothes. First, it was the halter top that was choking the hell out of her breasts. When she took it off, I got a full view of her voluptuous double D breasts. She shook them in my face for more effect. I was just standing there with my hands across my chest and wondering what the protocol was for having titties in my face. She then turned around and assumed the position on the hood as if I was a cop getting ready to search, the only problem was that my view was obstructed by her pink cookies and I realized that I was a man after all. My dick sprung up through my pants and I couldn't hide it from Kendra. She stood there with victory written on her face, a contemptuous smile and said, "You're gonna be a good boy and give me what I want tonight, right?"   I was looking at her like she was crazy, but when she leaned back on the car, pulled up her skirt and started playing with her clit, I felt the window of opportunity of having a choice in the situation was dwindling. She looked hot as hell and at that point I forgot my position on the situation. I wanted to get between her legs and start eating her. I was sure she could read my body language as she said, "Come here big boy and taste me." I was in zombie mode as I approached the car, knelt down and started eating Kendra. Her pussy was clean and it tasted good. She grabbed on to my hair as loud moans and groans escaped her mouth. "You're eating me so well," she cooed. Never one to leave a job half done, especially sex, I spread apart Kendra's legs as I found myself enjoying the taste of her nectar. The fear that I once had for this woman suddenly started to egress from the confines of my mind.

If I didn't have a choice as to whether or not the future of my marriage relied on me playing this woman's game, I figured I may as well enjoy it. Kendra and I switched positions as I took post on the hood of the car while she knelt between my legs and started to deep throat my long dick. "You have a beautiful dick," she said while licking her way up and down my shaft. "You like this dick? Suck it. And suck it good," I told her as I grabbed a chunk of her hair from the back of her head to reinforce my authority. My dick was in the back of her throat and she was enjoying every minute of it. "I like a forceful man," she said in between licks. 'Shut the hell up and suck my dick like a good girl is supposed to," I told her. "Yes, daddy," she responded. I hate to say it, but Kendra gave a mean blowjob. My pants was halfway down my thigh when she was sucking me, but I needed to take them completely off for comfort. As I reached down to pull my pants off, Kendra decided to give me a helping hand. First, she eased my shoes off my feet and then slowly pulled my pants off one leg at a time without ever allowing my dick to leave her mouth.

Her pink pussy was calling me and I wanted to fuck the hell out of her once and for all. "Stand up," I commanded. She stood up and placed her hands on the hood of the car. I didn't even think about it, I just plowed my dick into her pussy from the back without as much as thinking about putting on a condom. Her pussy felt nice, tight and moist. My first few strokes were slow. I wanted to enjoy her pussy. "Oh yes, fuck me slow, daddy," she cooed. Her supple honey skin felt great as I palmed her ass. The view from the back was magnificent as my dick went in and out Kendra's pussy. "Oh yeah," I said without realizing how much I had gotten into fucking her. Never once did I think about the possibility of catching a disease or this woman getting pregnant by me, which was foolish. I started to violently smack her ass as my strokes became stronger, longer and more forceful. "Fuck me, daddy! I like that! Fuck me hard!" she screamed. Her screams only fueled my will to make her submit to my prowess. I fucked her harder and harder until it became too hot in the garage. "I want you to turn around and get on your back," I ordered. She was now lying on her back with her legs spread apart and I could see her erected clit just calling for attention. After I inserted my dick inside her pussy, I proceeded to rub her clit while I pounded her pussy. I had one hand on her clit, one on her breast and my dick satisfying the hell out of her. It was a beautiful scene. I fucked Kendra's gorgeous ass until she begged for mercy. She came so many times, her pussy became sensitive. I came once all over her ass. She had to go in the house to wipe it off her butt.

Satisfied with my performance, I had Kendra believing that I was all about her on the ride back to my hotel to drop me off. "You know I'm really starting to like you. We're gonna have to find a way to keep this a secret from my wife until things can be worked out," I told her. "I'm so happy that we're finally going to be together you just don't know. Baby, you are a stallion in the sack. I have never been fucked that way in my life. You're mine to keep," she said. A part of me wanted to chuckle inside, while another part of me became scared of her latter statement. I told Kendra that I needed to get some sleep so I could get up early enough for my flight and she understood. She dropped me off and promised to call me when she got back home.

After Kendra dropped me off at the hotel, I was confident that I could control the situation with my dick. I needed to have her under the spell of good sex and that's what I planned on using to keep her at bay while I sorted out a solution to my problem. Be as it may, I truly enjoyed fucking Kendra, but I didn't want to be with her. I valued my family more.

Hello, Good Morning

I hadn't talked to my wife and kids since the previous day and I needed to check in to let them know that I was okay. I was also missing them and I needed to hear their voices for comfort. My wife was like Sherlock Holmes in a skirt. She always knew when something was wrong with me without me having to tell her. I needed to be careful not to raise any suspicion while talking to her. I decided not to call the night before when I came in because it was so late and I didn't want her to smell Kendra's pussy on my breath over the phone. She's that good. She could detect smells from Africa while sitting in her living room in America. Not only that, I was feeling guilty as sin because I ended up enjoying having sex with Kendra.

Since my flight was scheduled to leave at 6:30 in the morning, I had to be up by 4:00AM to get ready. The drive to the airport from my hotel was about forty minutes to an hour and I needed to get to the airport an hour before departure, which was 5:30AM. The good thing about technology is that things can get done in a simpler and easier way. I decided to check into my flight online the night before. The fact that I always have my carry-on baggage with me always makes things a little easier as well. After I made it to the airport and through security, I still had about thirty minutes before I boarded my flight. It was at that time I decided to call my wife to tell her I was on my way home. I knew it was rather early to call, but I had a good hunch that my son had already awoken her anyway.

"Good morning, Sunshine," I said after hearing her voice. "Hi, baby. How come I haven't heard from you in the last couple of days?" she asked with concern in her tone. My wife has always understood that I get extremely busy when I go on tour. She's always tried her best not to bother me too much with the phone calls. I appreciated her for that, but I also always make it a point to call her at least a couple of times a day. I was quickly trying to figure out a good answer. "Things got real hectic. I was running from one signing to the next and before I knew it, I lost track of time. I thought it would be unfair to call you late because you hardly get any rest with the kids during the day. I'm sorry, baby," I said trying to sound as sincere as possible. "Well you know I'm not the only person that you need to check on. You've got three little ones here too. Just come home safe and I'll see you when you get here," she said anticipating my arrival.

Normally, I would have my wife drop me off at the airport. However, because she would have to haul the children with her, I would always drive myself and leave my car in the parking lot. I sat at the airport reflecting on the events of the previous night and I was frightened by my actions. Not only did I have unprotected sex with a lunatic, I actually let my guard down and allowed myself to get into the act. I had no idea where Kendra's antics were going next, but I was sure to stay on my toes to keep it all from my wife. I was guilt ridden and felt bad that I had cheated on her. Coming clean to my wife was not an option because it would devastate her. At least, that's what I wanted to tell myself for my own sake. I knew it was a selfish act, but I wasn't willing to act selfless to resolve it without causing pain to my wife. When they finally called passengers to board, I almost felt like going home to face my wife. My guilt was written all over my face and the betrayal that I caused was going to eat at my heart for a long time.

After I boarded, I went to the middle of the plane and took my seat next to the window. Though I was happy to leave Atlanta, I wasn't sure what would transpire when I got home. Normally, I would put on my glasses and catch some ZZZs while on the plane, but I couldn't keep my eyes close. I was also nervous at the sight of one particular woman rushing to board the plane last minute. She sat in first class. I couldn't really make out her face, but her side profile was very close to Kendra's. No way would she try to come to Boston with her bullshit, I thought. She wasn't crazy enough to bring that shit into my backyard. Besides, we had a deal and I fucked her well enough to make her believe that things would work out as long as she stayed away from my family.

Feeling Antsy

The idea of Kendra possibly being on that plane dominated my every thought. I needed confirmation. I wanted to walk up to first class to see who that woman was, but the curtain that separated the important people in first class from the common folks in the back prevented me from getting a good view of her. What could they do if I pulled the curtain and walked right up there? Would it cause a scene? I sure as hell didn't want a scene on my account. I also didn't want to sit through a three-hour flight without finding out if the woman was indeed Kendra. I had to figure out a way to get to first class. The plane was full without an empty seat anywhere. The nosey folks kept their eyes on anyone who got up to use the bathroom or walk down the aisle. I didn't want to be stared at, but I needed information on the woman. I got up and attempted to walk toward the front to act like I was going to use the restroom in first class when a line started forming near the bathroom in the back. However, I was quickly halted by the airline steward who told me, "Sir, the restroom in the front is for first class customers only." I didn't want to make a fuss, so I went back to my seat.

During the plane home I was trying to force myself to sleep, but I couldn't because I kept seeing the ghost of Kendra on the plane. My biggest fear was that she would eventually bring this shit to my front door. My eyes shuddered for but a few minutes, I thought, and it was the best nap that I could've asked for until…I saw Kendra in my bedroom at home tied to the bedpost and I had a whip in my hand while working on her. "Are you gonna be a good girl, or do I have to spank you to goodness?" I asked while dreaming about her. "I want you to discipline me, daddy. I've been a bad girl," she said. She was wearing a leather thong, leather bra and a leather eye mask over her eyes. I was shirtless wearing a pair of boy-fitted briefs. Kendra was lying on her stomach while she stuck her ass out awaiting the connection of the whip to her ass. "I love it when you're rough with me, daddy. Spank me!" she said in a seductive voice. I raised my hand high and softly allowed the whip to land on her buttocks. "Spank me harder, daddy!" she screamed once more. I added a little more force to my swing and let loose the leather whip across her ass. Red marks soon appeared and she started begging for more pain. I guess even in my dreams this woman was crazy.

"I didn't mean to kill your wife, daddy. I'm sorry. Punish me some more," she said. I may have been dreaming, but it was some disturbing shit to hear her say that she didn't mean to kill my wife. What was even more disturbing was the fact that I said to her, "I told you to get rid of her, not kill her." At this point it was no longer a dream. It had become a nightmare. I woke up sweating and mumbling words to myself that the other passengers couldn't make out. The flight attendant came over to ask me if I was okay. It was then that I realized I was still sitting on the plane and the captain announced that we would be landing in a few minutes. I was so happy that it was just a dream. I thought this chick killed my wife.

Now, I definitely needed to know if that person was Kendra on the plane. However, I still faced the hurdle of trying to get to the front of the plane to confirm her identity. Getting around it was hard because the flight was sold out. I couldn't move my seat up. And I knew that Kendra would be off the plane by the time I reached the front door when the plane landed. The one time that I should have flown first class, I didn't. Finally the plane landed and we were at the gate. The minute the interior lights came on, I tried to make a dash for the front, but my efforts were futile as anxious passengers impatiently got up to position themselves for an early exit off the plane. I even left my baggage behind. I just wanted to see who the woman was. There must've been at least fifty people ahead of me and I knew for sure that I would be able to identify the woman. What made it even worse was the fact that the flight attendant never pulled back the curtain that separated the first class section from the coach section.

As anxious as I was to find out if Kendra was indeed on the plane, I felt defeated because she was long gone by the time I deplaned. I went down to baggage claim to see if she might have been in the waiting area, but no luck. I immediately called my wife to tell her that my plane landed and I was on my way home. I also asked her to make sure that all the doors were locked, which I'm sure sounded kind of strange. I was already digging a hole for myself.

Paranoia

After talking to my wife about our lives, marriage and children, she re-affirmed my belief that I was in jeopardy of losing my family if she had any inclination of infidelity. She told me that she would leave me without a second thought if I ever cheated on her. Her heart couldn't take the pain of another man cheating on her. I didn't want to wake a sleeping dog, but I had to remind her that she was cheating on her husband with me when I met her. At that point, her answer was, "I only cheated on him because he was cheating on me and was also physically abusing me." I shouldn't have ever brought that up. Looking for a justification for my behavior almost put me at odds with my wife. "Baby, I would never cheat on you, anyway. I was just curious about the foundation and strength our relationship," I lied.

Though it was Sunday morning, I still needed a different perspective in order to deal with my predicament justly. I contemplated getting Kevin involved but at the end of the day his loyalty would most likely lie with his sister. I did the next best logical thing; I called Rammel to ask him to meet me in the office. When he picked up the phone, I could immediately tell that he had a woman over. I had to wait until Monday to meet with Rammel because he had plans to smash this cutie all day on Sunday. Besides, I didn't want to talk on the phone in the house about the situation, anyway. I went about my day trying my best not to trip myself up to my wife. I kept thinking that Kendra was going to show up at the house with a large envelop with pictures of me and her having sex and handing it to my wife. I felt that nothing was beneath her and she would go to any length to get what she wanted.

I ended up spending most of the day with my children in the house. Most of the time when we have nice weather I would take the kids out to the park for some type of outdoor activity, but I didn't want to leave the house in case Kendra showed up. "It's a nice day honey, why don't you take the kids to the park like you usually do?" my wife asked. "I'm not in the mood for the park, baby. I just want to stay home with them and make this a relaxing day with the family. You know I missed you as well, so I get to be around all the people I love," I told her. Sunday is a special day in our household. My wife always cooked a big meal and made sure that we sat down at the dinner table to eat as a family. "Well you know I'll be preparing dinner today, so you're gonna have to keep the kids out of my way," she requested. "I will, baby. I'm gonna take them downstairs to the play room with me," I told her. "You know, when was the last time I gave my wife a passionate kiss and told her that I loved her?" I said while staring and smiling at my wife. "I think that doesn't happen enough, so you better get on it. Come get that kiss and tell me how much you love your slaving wife. You know I'mma be slaving over that stove today," she playfully said. I gave her a long kiss and reassured her that she was the only woman in my life.

I spent the day in the basement with the kids, playing with them, but more importantly I kept my eyes focused on the front entrance of my house. I could see the entrance from the basement window and I wanted to make sure that I could intervene in case crazy-ass Kendra decided to show up. Even my little girl kept asking, "Daddy, why you keep staring at the window?" I really had to make it part of our game so I told her, "Daddy wants to make sure the monster doesn't come to the house to take my babies." The game room as well as the family room was down in the basement. I watched television with my kids. They especially liked Nickelodeon. Every time the door bell rang on the television, I thought it was the door bell to my house and my stomach knotted. I would try to run up the stairs to answer it before my daughter said, "Daddy, that was the door bell on the television." I was looking foolish, but we made a game of it. The kids and I were downstairs in the basement for a while playing Hop Scotch and all kinds of other imaginary games. Finally, my wife called to tell us that dinner was ready.

As is customary, we went and washed our hands and took our seat at the table in the dining room to show our appreciation to my wife for her hard work in the kitchen. After my little girl said grace, the feasting began. My wife made stewed chicken, rice and peas, macaroni and cheese, fried plantain, steamed vegetables and biscuits. My wife watched the cooking channel whenever she had time and we got a chance to benefit from her cooking adventures every Sunday. On this particular Sunday, she decided to give us a Jamaican treat. My children and I more than enjoyed the meal.

After dinner, I was still ridden with guilt, but I wanted things to be as normal as possible. I decided to watch the late football game on Sunday night. I knew my wife was a little tired from cooking all day, but because of my guilt, I wanted to make love to her to make her feel like she was the only woman in the world to me. My attempt failed because she was knocked out by the time I entered the room to go to bed. I hardly got any sleep that night. I tossed and turned all night. I couldn't wait until the next day to go have that conversation with Rammel.

Me and the Homies

I got up bright and early that morning. I did my routine work out in my home gym. Normally, I would make good use of my gym membership at Bally's, but I was amped up and needed to release some stress. Since it was still early, I also decided to make the best use of my time by getting my invoices ready for Borders and Ingram for the following month. Though I was worried that Kendra might show up to my house, I couldn't get to the office fast enough to meet with Rammel so we could talk. I wanted him to be there at 9:00 AM sharp, so I placed another call to him as a reminder.

After I arrived in the office, my nosey receptionist was asking me all kinds of questions about the trip over the weekend. Normally, I would entertain her questions a little, but on this day I was in no mood for it. Of course, it had nothing to do it with her; it was more my guilt getting the best of me. She was always more excited to hear about my trips than she was nosey. I didn't want to give her the cold shoulder on purpose, but I did. The inviting personality that I usually carried disappeared that day. Rammel hadn't made it in yet, so I went into my office and shut the door. I wanted to focus on my work and the company, but I couldn't bring myself to do any work, or even think for that matter. I was consumed by my situation and I had no one to blame but me for putting myself in that situation. Whether it was curiosity or just the allure of being in the company of a beautiful woman, I should've just stayed in my lane.

When Rammel finally showed up thirty minutes later, I decided to take him on a ride with me to Franklin Park because I didn't want to risk my receptionist hearing any part of my conversation. While in the car, I explained the entire situation to him. "Yo, that broad is crazy. You need to come up with a plan to get rid of her ass," he said. "I know that, stupid. Why do you think I'm telling you about it? I need your help to come up with a plan. As fine as she is, she's the ugliest woman in the world to me right now," I said to him. "I can dig it. After everything you told me, I probably would've choked her ass. I'm not sure if it's a good idea to tell Kevin, though," he cautioned. While Rammel and I tried to figure out the best course of action to deal with the situation, Kevin called me and wanted to meet in the office to discuss the promotional plans for his next book. "Yo, meet me at the office in a couple of hours. I'm taking care of something with Rammel right now. Peace," I quickly hung up the phone and told Rammel that was Kevin. "Yo Dave, I would try to keep that shit as far away from Kevin as possible. You know how Kevin can be all protective of his sister. But we still gotta come up with a plan to get rid of this chick," Rammel reminded me. "I know. I just hope she wasn't the woman on the plane, man, cause I don't know how I'mma deal with that," I said sadly. "Man, we're gonna deal with it the best way we can. We ain't gonna have no woman come and wreck what we got going on here. Marsha is a big part of this company, and if you split with her, it might fuck up the business. I ain't trying to have some broad take food away from me, so we're gonna have to deal with her," Rammel said supportively.

I never really quite thought of it the way Rammel did, but Kendra was going to affect the livelihood of all of us. My wife was an integral part of the company's growth. Though she worked from home, she was very effective in making sure the word got out about all of our releases, events and overall marketing. She wrote our monthly newsletter and gathered the info for our email and mailing list. All of that would go down the tube if my marriage failed. I needed to take a whole different approach to the situation. It wasn't just the home front that was going to be affected, but my life as a whole.

When Rammel and I made it back to the office, Kevin was standing at the front flirting with the receptionist as usual. The sexual tension between the two of them was at an all time high. Kevin was the sought-after thug writer that every chick in the hood wanted to sleep with and my receptionist was the reserved, former private school girl who dreamed about getting turned out by a bad boy. She would often ask whether the events in his book were a part of his life. She was intrigued by his bad boy demeanor, saggy jeans, oversized t-shirt, Timberland books and the big ass diamond medallion he bought when he first got his advance. I also believed that Kevin never really left the streets alone. I knew he was a hustler and moved plenty copies of his book, but he didn't make enough money to be driving around in that black BMW 645 coupe he was in. However, he was able to mask his street hustling due the success of his book. Kayla, my receptionist, would get all giddy and lost whenever Kevin showed up at the office. I will be ready the day that I step in my office to find her legs spread across my desk while Kevin takes her to seventh heaven. It was always an expectation of mine, anyway.

Rammel and I signaled for Kevin to join us in the adjoining conference room so we could discuss the marketing and promotion of his new book. He had done a good job on the street with his guerilla and grassroots marketing, but now it was time to get him the national fanfare that the book needed to top his last release. Kevin was good about getting everybody around him involved with his promotions. His flyers were being handed out at every train station, the posters for his new book were everywhere, his MySpace and Facebook book friends were being blasted and reminded at least once a week about the book. All the women who wanted to be down with him were involved with his project. He catered to all their needs so they could cater to his. His success gave them bragging rights and he was promising monogamy to all of them. He was the ultimate hustler.

"So Kev, how we gonna handle the promotions this time around? I know you want it bigger than last time," I said while chuckling. Kevin was a sure bet investment for me and after reading the sequel to his first book, I knew his audience would be left in awe, anticipating the last part of his trilogy. "I appreciate all the effort you put behind my book, but the goal is to move 10,000 copies out the gate within the first week. I got Boston on lock and we're working on Worcester, Springfield, Brockton and a few surrounding cities as well as Rhode Island and Connecticut. I also need to go to New York to link up with my connects on the streets in Harlem, Jamaica and Brooklyn. We're gonna kill them with this one," Kevin said with confidence. I liked his zeal and determination to succeed. Kevin was a mirror image of me when it came to promoting himself and his work. I didn't have to worry about his book flopping, which was one of the key interests in him as a person. I also couldn't afford to lose him as a friend and brother in law.

After meeting with Kevin and Rammel for about two hours to go over the logistics and demographics for the promotion of Kevin's new book, we decided to break for lunch. We went down to Lenny's bakery on Blue Hill Ave to enjoy their flavorful Jamaican menu. I had eaten enough of Marsha's Jamaican cuisine the night before, so I opted for the cocoa bread and cheese with the beef patty, while the fellas grubbed on oxtail and rice and curry chicken and rice. We all washed our food down with a Jamaican champagne cola. The whole time we were eating lunch was like a roast. We kept cracking on each other and for a moment, my mind drifted away from the Kendra situation as I enjoyed lunch with my boys.

The Unknown

I was gone most of the day trying to sort out my problems to save my marriage. When I got home that evening, my wife told me that a salesperson came to the house and was trying to sell her some kind of policy. At first she didn't tell me whether it was a man or a woman, but as the conversation about the strange salesperson lingered, she revealed it was a woman. Though it wasn't unusual for door-to-door salesman to come to my neighborhood attempting to hook us with some kind of product, I found it rather strange that one would show up at my door step the day after I thought I noticed Kendra on the plane. "What was she trying to sell you?" I asked casually. I had to be careful and I needed to proceed with caution so that I wouldn't raise my wife's suspicion to anything. "She was just trying to sell me some life insurance. She told me that I may need it when I least expect it because tomorrow's not promised," my wife told me. "What did she mean by that?" I asked hesitantly. "I don't know what she meant, but she said that it was important to have the insurance in case something happened to me. She wanted to make sure you would have enough money to hire a nanny to help care for my kids," my wife told me.

My suspicions were confirmed. How dare she?! I said silently to myself. She was playing dirty by bringing this shit to my door step. I still couldn't show my emotions. I didn't want my wife to be suspicious at all. "Did she mention that I needed to get the insurance in case something happened to me, so you and my children could be ok?" I asked. My wife looked at me and her eyes lit up because she thought I was being considerate. A smile flashed across her face at the thought of me providing security for my family and then said, "No. She didn't suggest it at all." I tried my best to look at my wife in the most sincere way and told her, "Well, you know I bought a two-million dollar policy for the family in case anything ever happened to me. I also purchase insurance to pay off the home should I fall ill or die prematurely. You and the kids are taken care of." My wife just smiled and pulled me towards her for a kiss. "Enough about the woman; how was your day at the office today?" she asked, forcing me to change the subject. "My day was fine. I just have a few things to iron out for Kevin's next book and the other releases for the fall," I told her. I couldn't keep my daughter from wrapping herself around my leg, something I had grown accustomed to and loved.

Every time I came home, my daughter would run to me and stayed next to me until it was time for her to go to bed. No way was I going to give that up for Kendra.

I was sitting on the couch with my daughter, but my mind was floating somewhere else. I didn't want to have pity on myself, but my situation was stressful and I stood to lose the thing I enjoyed most in my life at the time, my family. Now I was thinking all bets were off. Kendra may have just pushed me to the point of no return. The nice guy within was about to evacuate. I was now having thoughts that correlated more to the idea of keeping my family intact. They were becoming deadly thoughts, even. Kendra had to go and I needed to find a way to wipe off all traces of my presence in her life before I did anything.

I was hoping to confirm the identity of the woman who showed up at my house, but there was no segue back into that conversation, since my wife decided to change the subject. Now I had to torment myself to figure out who the hell came to my house and who in the world was on that plane.

Surprise!

I had been so caught up with my web of deception that it took Kevin to remind that my little girl's birthday was coming up in a week. "Yo Dave, since Savant has a birthday coming up, what do you think I should get her this year as a present?" Kevin asked. It was then that I remembered my daughter's 5th birthday was in a couple of weeks. My mind was just preoccupied with so much drama I neglected to plan something special for the people most special in my life. "Damn man, I had promised Savant a party for her birthday," I said out loud. "Why you acting like it's too late to plan it? It's still nice out, we can have a cookout for her," Kevin suggested. A cook-out would be ideal since my daughter was born in September. The New England weather would be perfect and I wouldn't have to do too much planning. First, I needed to get on the phone to call my wife to tell her that I had promised Savant a party for her birthday. My wife picked up the phone on the second ring, "Babe, I meant to tell you that I promised Savant a party for her birthday. Can you please call her friends to let them know that we're having a cookout next Saturday?" I told my wife. "Dave, don't you think that's a little short notice? I wish you had made me aware of this a few weeks ago so I could've planned it accordingly," she said almost in a disapproving tone. "Babe, it's not a big deal. We're gonna throw a surprise party for her. It doesn't have to be a big shindig. Call everybody, whoever can attend we will be happy to have, and those who can't make will miss a great party. You might wanna start putting together your shopping list. I love you. Bye," I said quickly before hanging up the phone because I could only imagine my wife's screw face at me.

"I guess the party's at my house next Saturday. Bring someone special, fellas," I said to my boys. Kevin quickly tried to hush me because he didn't want Kayla to know about the party. Kevin wasn't the type to bring a woman anywhere because he was always on the hunt for new pussy. The last thing he wanted was for Kayla to be hanging around him all night at a party. Kevin was Savant's godfather and he cherished my daughter as if she was his own. He was always bringing gift items to the house for her. He was the type of uncle who could spoil a child and make the parents feel as if they weren't doing enough. My wife and I understood that was his personality, so we never took it away from him. It was set. My daughter's actual birthday was on Monday, but it made more sense to have the party on Saturday.

One of the reasons my wife was a little upset with me about giving my daughter a party was because she knew she was gonna be the one who was going to do everything. I was always good on promises, but short on planning. I delivered every time, but my wife always played a big role in putting it all together. We were a team. I didn't always contribute my share, but nonetheless we were still a team. I knew all of my shortcomings and my wife knew them too. I probably had more shortcomings than Marsha, but I knew how to make up for it. That day happened to be one of those days that I needed to make up for it. I had to get a move on because I knew the horns would be out when I got home. I gave dap to my boys and made my walk down to the florist on Walk Hill and American Legion highway to buy a dozen roses for my wife. I also made a quick stop to the mall in Braintree to buy a pearl necklace that I noticed she was fascinated with while looking through one of those catalogs from Zales.

With my roses in hands and the pearl necklace wrapped in a nice box with a bow around it, I was ready to face the music at home. As usual, I would stop by the mail box to pick up the mail before I go into house. However, on this day, I noticed a yellow envelop with bright red lipstick marks all over it sitting on top of my regular mail. There was a stamp on the envelope like it had been delivered by the mailman. I looked around to make sure my wife wasn't looking at me through the shades. When I opened the envelope there was a card inside that read,

I know you're probably going to hate me for this, but I miss you and can't wait another day to see you. I didn't mean to come all the way to Boston to bother you, but I want to be close to my man. I understand you have to work things out with your wife, but my patience is growing thin. I need to be with my man. I'm also tired of sharing my man with another woman.

Your True Love,

Kendra

After reading the last line in the letter, I took it as a threat to my wife and family. Something was going to have to be done sooner rather than later. There I was in the midst of planning a party to celebrate my baby girl's birthday and this lunatic woman was lurking around waiting to spoil my plans. The enthusiasm and energy that I had before going to the mailbox was deflated. I still carried the roses and gift to my wife with the same fervor, but I was worried inside. I didn't know if I could deal with this much longer. I had no idea how long I was going to have my family around me if this situation persisted.

I tried to walk though the house as nonchalant and as apologetic as I could as I handed my wife the roses and the gift I bought for her. She reluctantly gave me a kiss, because she knew I was trying to buy my way out of the dog house. Again my little girl was wrapped around my legs the moment she noticed me. Again I was sitting on the couch holding my little girl and contemplating my plans to rid myself of this pain-in-the-ass woman. The life that I had was everything that I dreamed having a family would be. I was happy and my willingness to fight for that happiness ran deep in my bones.

Now it was a race to get to the mailbox before my wife did after I received that card from Kendra. I wanted to call so badly, but I figured it wouldn't do me any good. It would just add fuel to whatever purpose she thought she served in my life. I negated the whole thing by avoiding her. I was hoping after long enough she would get the picture and go on her merry way. I later found out that my idea would be fruitless.

The week couldn't go by fast enough. I needed to refocus on the good things that were happening in my life. I decided to put all my energy into helping my wife plan my daughter's party. We kept the party from my daughter during the whole week, but she wouldn't stop reminding me that I had promised her a party. My daughter was so cute whenever she started talking about all the different types of entertainment she wanted at the party. The first order was to have her favorite cartoon character in a life size balloon in the backyard. I had to call so many places to get a life size Dora brought to the house. I also got a clown, and even thought about getting a pony for the party. Even though it was short notice, I wanted to give my daughter a party that she would never forget, even at five years old.

The day of the party finally came. I asked my parents to pick up Joseph and Daniella so I could get the backyard ready for the party while my wife took Savant with her to the beauty salon to pamper and keep her away from the party grounds. The tables were set, Dora was inflated, the clown confirmed and the food was ready for the grill. By the time my wife came home with my daughter, it was early evening and people had started to gather in the backyard. We kept the music off until my daughter arrived.

Most of her friends were able to come with their parents, except for maybe a couple. As planned, my wife blindfolded my daughter before bringing her to the backyard and placed her right next to the life-size inflatable Dora doll. Everyone kept quiet until my wife asked her to take off the blindfold, at which time everyone yelled, "Surprise!" My daughter was ecstatic to see her friends, Dora, a big cake with her name on it and lots of presents. We all sang happy birthday to her and the party continued.

Everyone was having a great for at least a couple of hours when Kevin decided to make his grand entrance. Rammel was already at the party gulping down a few beers and clowning around with the rest of our friends. I thought the biggest surprise was when my daughter found out about her party, but boy was I wrong. As always, Kevin liked a lot of attention and he marveled in it. It was no surprised when he came in with one of those convertible battery-operated Jeeps for my daughter that upstaged every gift she received that day. The Jeep was beautiful, but what was even more beautiful and surprising was the fact that Kevin came to the party with Kendra on his arm. I almost choked on my beer when I saw her. Initially, I wanted to run back inside my house, but I caught myself and decided to act like I didn't know her. Everyone was staring at the scantily clad beautiful woman who wore the shortest poom-poom shorts she could find in her closet, and the tightest little top to cover her breasts. Kevin should've known better to bring Kendra to a kid's party looking like a hoochie mama, but then again, Kevin was a flashy type of guy and he wanted the whole world to see his game.

Her Sneakiness

As Kevin went around introducing his new girl to everyone he knew at the party, I was wondering if I should act like I didn't already know Kendra. I decided to play off whatever she fed me. I tried my best to act like I had never seen her, but Kendra wouldn't have it that way. "Dave, this is my new girl Kandy. Kandy this is my boy, Dave," Kevin said as he introduced her to me. "Hi, I'm Kandy. You look like that author Dave Richardson. He's my favorite author of all time," Kendra said to me. "He don't just look like him. This is the one and only author Dave Richardson. World renowned," Kevin said with his bad boy flair. I could tell that Kevin hadn't slept with Kendra yet because he still had that hunger in his eyes. For now she had him under her spell, but in my mind, I was wondering what she was up to with Kevin. She had to have been trying to get at me, and using Kevin was the easiest way into my home. I knew I should've never written *The Bedroom Bandit*. I revealed too much information about my life in that book.

Since Rammel wasn't too far behind me, he extended his hand as well and said, "Where in the world did

Kevin find you? I need to move to that part of the world."

Of course, Kendra let her pearly whites flash across her face exposing a smile so perfect that even orthodontists wondered why she's not the spokesperson for Colgate. Rammel was salivating like a little boy. "A'ight, I'mma give you your props on that one. Can't none of us top this one," Rammel whispered to Kevin. Little did he know; I had already topped it and smack it and she was deranged. Kevin walked around with Kendra on his arm like she was a trophy.

That did it for me. She brought the drama to my home, at my daughter's birthday party at that. I needed to do something. My wife has always had good instincts, and her instincts had never been wrong. I went inside the house to get more ice and she followed behind me. Once she found me, she let off enough insults about that woman a machine gun couldn't keep up with her speed, "Why did Kevin bring that harlot to my home? He can't see she's one of those money hungry harlots who probably want him for the little money he has? She's got skank written all over her and I don't want her to step foot inside my house. Keep her in the back." She went on and on and I said nothing. I just nodded my head in agreement every time our eyes met. The venom that came out of my wife's mouth about Kendra was so foul,

I wondered what she would do if she found out that I had been with Kendra. Now I was also starting to wonder if her name was really Kendra because she came in with Kevin introducing herself as Kandy. Kevin was sure to let everyone know it was Kandy with a "K." That shit was funny.

I almost wanted to smack Rammel upside the head because he kept rambling on about how fine Kendra was. That fool was blinded by beauty and a big booty. I knew I couldn't tell him that Kandy was actually Kendra, the woman that I had been telling him about. I didn't want hysteria to break out because Rammel couldn't contain himself. If ever he wished he was Kevin, this was the day and time. I think most of the men who were there that day sort of wished they were Kevin for that day. I never could understand the impact that a beautiful woman could have on men. Most of us are like putty in the hands of a beautiful woman. I guess I was no different because when I first met Kendra, I was mesmerized by her beauty as well, and that's what led to the situation that I was in.

Kevin finally decided to set Kendra down in a chair while he prepared a plate for her. She was smirking the whole time while looking at me because she felt she had me by the balls. I wanted to wipe that smirk off her face, but I had to be patient. My turn would come soon. While Kendra was sitting in the corner picking through her plates, Kevin decided to come to me and Rammel to get more accolades from us about his new girl. "Yo, shawty is fine as hell. I think I'mma keep this one," Kevin bragged. "You said that about the last girl you pulled. You're basing your decision to keep a woman strictly on her looks, that's not good. What if she's a lunatic?" I said casually. "Yo, fuck that, I know that I would go loony on that ass," Rammel said as he tapped Kevin. He was still sweating Kevin's nuts and I was irritated by it. I wanted to tell them so badly about this chick so they could both shut the fuck up. She was not worth all that praise they were bestowing upon her. "I'mma take my time to hit that and make sure she falls in love with my shit," Kevin continued to brag. "Just be careful. All that glitters ain't gold," I told him. "Dave, that's some hater-ade shit coming out your mouth right there. I thought you'd be happy for me, bro," Kevin said with disappointment. "Man, I'm tripping. Of course, I'm happy for you. Just make sure she's the right one before you rush into anything," I said almost in a commending kind of way. "Shawty looks like she's missing me already. Let me get back to her," Kevin said before walking back to where Kendra was sitting. I didn't want to hear Rammel's mouth anymore about this woman, so I just walked away from him after Kevin left.

Meanwhile, Kendra kept winking and smiling at me whenever she thought no one was looking. She might have been amusing herself, but I was not amused at all. I almost felt like asking her to leave. However, just when I felt like she had just pushed all the buttons she could push, she reached for yet another one. Kevin walked up to Marsha and asked if Kendra could use the bathroom. I knew my wife didn't want her in the house but she had to be cordial to her brother's friend. She told Kendra to follow her to the bathroom in the basement that we had set up for our guests. My wife left her in the bathroom to continue on with her business. Kendra seemed like she was taking forever to come out the bathroom. I wondered if this nutty chick was inside my house doing something crazy. I went inside to check on her to make sure she didn't sneak upstairs or was walking around my house snooping through my family's belongings. "Kendra, are you ok?" I asked as my foot reached the last step to the basement. I called out her name again and no answer. Finally as I got closer to the bathroom, I noticed that the door was opened. She emerged from behind the door and tried to pin me up for a kiss. Kendra must've been nuts, but she had no idea what kind of an ass-whipping Marsha would put on her if she caught her kissing me in her house. Marsha was twice as crazy. My first reaction was to step back immediately and loosened myself up from her grip. "Now you wanna act like you don't want me?" she said in teasing manner. "What the fuck are you doing here? Do you know today is my daughter's birthday? I will knock your ass dead if you mess up my daughter's special day," I threatened her. "That's not the reason why I'm here. I missed my man and wanted to see him. I don't care about your daughter's little birthday party. I'm here for you," she said. I was infuriated and wanted so much to react violently, but I couldn't. "Look, get your shit together and get the fuck outta my house before I drag your ass out. I'm not up for your little game and you've taken this shit too far," I said sternly. "No motherfucker, you took it too far when you decided to fuck me and thought you could just walk away from me. You ain't gonna fuck with my emotions and just leave me hanging that ain't happening. I'll get out of your little house, but you best believe that you're not gonna get rid of me that easily," she threatened.

I stormed out the house before she pushed me to do something that I would regret to her trifling ass. I went back to be the attentive daddy that I needed to be to my little girl.

Kendra was no longer the focus of the party as more people started to arrive and the party started to take on a life of its own. The music was jumping courtesy of one of Boston's hottest DJs. People were dancing and having a good time. Kevin sheltered Kendra that entire night while she sat in her chair. The honored guest of the party fell asleep in my arms around eleven o'clock along with her brother and sister. I was happy when the party finally ended. My wife and I had a lot clean up to do, but it was all worth it. Rammel stayed behind to help us clean and I had to keep hushing him whenever he brought up Kendra in front of my wife. Kevin also offered to help us clean, but my wife quickly declined his offer because she couldn't stand the sight of Kendra for another minute.

Plan of Action

After cleaning up behind the guests that evening, I was tired. I took a hot shower and expected to be knocked out almost immediately when my head touched my pillow, but I couldn't sleep. I kept racking my brain for a solution to rid myself of Kendra and I just couldn't come up with one. I knew she was using Kevin to get to me, and I wondered about the gist of her plans. I couldn't wait to be reactionary, I had to be proactive. I realized that night that too much thinking can also bring on a painful headache. I had to take some Nyquil to force myself to sleep. My problem, however, would still be present when I woke up in the morning and what bothered me the most.

I woke up bright and early the next day and went through the routine of my exercises at the house. I didn't want to leave my house fearing that Kendra might come back to do something to my wife and children. Or worst, I thought she might mail the proofs of us having sex to my wife. That thought alone kept me home. I couldn't even do any work because I could not focus. I even cancelled part of my tour until I figured out a way to get rid of Kendra. I felt like my whole world was being turned upside down because of my own stupidity. I felt like I was caught slipping and there was no way to rebound back. While I was downstairs racking my brains, my cell phone rang. I never expected to get a call from Kendra because she hadn't called me since I got back, but I expected nothing but bad news from her. It was just a matter of bracing myself for what was to come. I saved her number under the initial KD in case my wife ever went through my phone. For all she knew KD could be Kevin. Anyway, I reluctantly picked up the phone and the first thing out of Kendra's mouth was, "Hi baby. Have you checked your email? I've got something special for you there." I had no idea what the heck she was talking about so I tried my best to give her the cold shoulder. "Is there something that you specifically need? I see you've got a new boyfriend, so it shouldn't be a problem for you to let me go now. Bye." I hung up the phone before she got a chance to say anything. Kendra wouldn't give up that easily. She called me right back, but this time I sent the call to my voicemail.

I wanted to go to my office to see what it was that Kendra had sent to my email. I figured she obtained my public email from my book, because I never gave her my personal email address. I logged onto my computer anticipating yet another headache from Kendra, but this time was worst than I expected. Kendra emailed me what looked like it could be a Youtube link of us having sex on top of her car in the garage. That conniving tramp recorded the entire session in her garage. And in the email she wrote, *"I can either send a copy of it to your wife or it can be uploaded on Youtube for the whole family. I never lose. You better straighten up your act."* At that point, I felt like she was squeezing the hell out of my balls. I had to make her believe I was gonna leave my wife for her. Not one to incriminate myself by sending an email to Kendra, I went back downstairs to call her and tell that we needed to meet later that day.

We made plans to meet downtown on Park Street at 8:00PM. At first, Kendra suggested that I come to the hotel where she was staying, but I didn't want to be seen with her like that. She was staying at the Park Plaza hotel on Boylston street near Park Street, which was one of the reason I asked her to meet me there. I'm sure she thought she would be able to manipulate the situation to get me back to her room. However, I had other plans. Since I didn't have a gun, I knew who I needed to call to get my hands on one. I was going to get rid of Kendra once and for all. I wanted to meet her downtown then drive her to an isolated area in the woods near Houghton's Pond to put a bullet in her head. I was determined and willing to get rid of this woman once and for all.

Kevin

I didn't know too many people with street connections other than Kevin. I placed a call to him and asked him to meet me in the office because I needed to talk to him. I went and took a shower, got dressed and headed out the door. I was sure that Kendra wouldn't come to my house because we made plans to meet later. As I was pulling up to the office, I noticed Kevin was getting out of his car. I signaled for him to get in my car so we could go for a drive. I really didn't wanna talk about getting a gun from him in my office. "What up, big boy?" Kevin said with a big grin across his face. "What the fuck are you so happy about?" I asked. "Yo, I almost tapped that ass last night, but she let me eat her pussy. That shit was the bomb. She didn't want me to hit so soon because she said she want it to be special. I think I'mma make her my girl. Shawty's fine, smart and classy. What the fuck else can a man want?" he said trying to convince himself that Kendra was the woman for him. I just looked at him and shook my head. Only if he knew about the devil?

Since Kevin was gleeful about getting ass from Kendra and was more than happy to share the experience, I figured I'd pry for some information. "Yo Kev, where'd you meet that woman, man?" I asked casually. "Man, I met her while I was at Frugal Books doing a signing. I didn't even rap to her. Shawty came to me and told me she was a fan," he said feeling himself a little too much. "Did she buy your book?" I asked. "Nah, she was too fine to spend her money. I gave her one from my stack after I got her number," he said. "Had she read your book prior to coming to the signing?" I asked to raise his eyebrows. "She hadn't read it, but she said she gonna read it, though," he told, not totally sure of himself. "How the fuck is she a fan when she hadn't read the only book you wrote? That chick is just a groupie, man," I said. Even though my statement hit home with Kevin, he still didn't resonate with the fact. "Man, why you hatin' on my shine? You think you're the only one who got fans? I got fly chicks jocking me just like you do," he said with an angry tone. "If you got fly chicks jocking you, why you wanna keep this one? What's so special about her?' I asked, forcing him to think about his action and decision. "You must've forgotten how fine this chick was. I came up with one. Plus she's a doctor. It don't get better than that," Kevin said trying to convince himself he had pulled the cream of the crop. I started to ask myself if Kendra played me from the very beginning like she was playing Kevin. She told me she was a lawyer and told him she was a doctor. She was running game.

"I didn't know she was a doctor. I guess you came up. Just be careful and take your time with her," I cautioned. "Dave man, I think she's the one. I can see myself settling down with a woman like her, man. She's everything a man can dream of and more. Where else am I gonna find a doctor that fine?" Kevin kept saying. I wasn't sure if he was trying to convince himself or me at that point, but I was going to show support so I wouldn't appear as a hater. "I'm sure you know what you're doing. As long as you're happy, that's all that matters," I told him. "I am happy. I can't wait to see her again later. I can spend everyday with her and be happy. This delusional Negro was out of his mind. He barely knew Kendra and was already talking about a life with her. I looked at his gullible ass and laughed inside.

"Kev, one of the reasons I asked to see you is because I need you to get me a gun," I told him while I quickly hanged the subject. "A gun? You got beef with somebody? That ain't your ammo. Let me deal with that shit. You got three kids and a wife to worry about," Kevin offered. There was no way I was going to let this tramp bring Kevin into her web of deception, but I still needed to be careful with my approach as far as alerting Kevin about the true identity of Kendra and her motive. "Nah, it's nothing like that. I just have a situation and I will feel more secure if I'm packing. Ain't nothing like that gonna go down," I assured him. Of course, I was lying through my teeth and up to that point I had no idea if I had the courage to really kill Kendra. In the heat of the moment when I'm pent up with anger, I can do just about anything. "Dave, you sure you wanna pack heat? A lot of consequences come with that," Kevin cautiously warned. I thought about it for a minute and I decided that maybe I can scare the living shit out of Kendra if I put a gun to her head and threatened to blow her brains out if she came near my family. "I know the consequences. I need the gun. Are you gonna get me one or what?" I said in an annoying way. Kevin took a long look at me, reached behind his back and pulled what looked like the biggest revolver that I had ever seen and said, "Take this one." I was thinking to myself, *Goddamn! How the hell was I going to carry that gun?* I took a long look at the gun and said, "You got anything smaller?" He shook his head at me and said, "This is what I got right now, but I can get you one of them little .25's if that's what you want." I didn't really appreciate his sarcasm, but I wasn't ready to carry a big-ass gun. "Can you get at me later with the bitch-ass gun?" I asked in a serious tone. Kevin started laughing at me and said, "Real thugs don't ever walk around with just one gun. I gotta have something small to carry with me in the club." He opened a little hidden compartment in his car, pulled out a .25 caliber handgun and handed to me. "Make sure you wipe your prints off it, if you plan on using it. It's already loaded," he warned.

Damn, I had no idea how hard it was to be a thug. Carrying multiple guns and shit and having to worry about people trying to step up to you all the time, that couldn't be my life. I was shaking my head at Kevin as well, in a different way. "I know you're a grown- ass man and you wanna handle your business and all, but if you decide you don't wanna go through this and you need some help, just holler at me," Kevin offered once more. *If only he knew what I was planning on doing with the gun,* I said to myself. Instead of putting the gun around my waist, I decided to stick in my socks. That was only after Kevin schooled me on the safety aspects of carrying a gun. Now I was ready to put my plan in action and get rid of Kendra once and for all. "Yo Kev, I appreciate this, man. Please keep this between you and me. Marsha don't need to know that I borrowed a gun from you." I wanted to make sure Kevin didn't go back with his worries to my wife. "I got you," he said. I gave him dap, he hopped back in his car and left.

Round, Round I Go

When I left Kevin, I decided to run a few errands before I went back to the house. I almost forgot that I had a gun in my socks. I decided to place the gun in my glove compartment and locking it up with the key for safekeeping. I had to go see my boy Teryl Calloway at Calloway Graphix to get my promotional items printed and ready for the upcoming releases for the winter. Teryl has been the man who provided all my printing needs from the inception of my company. While growing up I heard stories about him being one the best promoters in the club game and one day we started kicking it and a business relationship ensued. My bookmarks, posters, banners, and stock cards have never looked so good thanks to Teryl. One of the perks of having him print those items was the turn-around time was always quick and I could just pick them up from his office in Boston without paying extra for shipping. Also, when I've needed something printed last minute, I could always count on Teryl.

I also stopped by my mother's house to check up on her. It had been a few days since I saw the love of my life. I needed to make sure she was okay. Seeing my mother always transformed me. She always knows how to lift my spirits and bring out the optimistic side of things. While sitting there talking to her I really wished that I could just tell her what was going on in my life with Kendra and the threat that it posed to my marriage, but I didn't want to disappoint her. My mom and I have always been close, but she held me in such high regards, I was ashamed to allow her to see that vulnerable and stupid side of me. I had disappointed her once in college and there was no way I would allow that to happen again if I didn't have to. We shared a few laughs over lemonade and she talked about how proud she was of me. And the fact that I decided not to become the same type of man my father was in her eyes, was just icing on the cake. My mother was most proud of the fact that I became a family man who took great care of my family. She couldn't stop singing my praises. I felt kind of guilty because I knew what was going on in my life and if my mother knew, she would put me in the same category as my dad. Not that my mother had ever said anything negative to me about my dad when I was a kid, but she insinuated that he wasn't always the best role model to me. After all, my dad was the one who left my mother for another woman and forgot that he left a child behind. I was just happy to make her proud, no matter what it took.

I also had to go see my uncle, Joe. It had been so long since I had seen him; I was almost ashamed to show up at his office in downtown Boston. Though my uncle supported my decision to marry Marsha, he wasn't in total agreement with it. He thought I was too young to marry. We occasionally met for basketball and baseball games, but it wasn't the same. Before we would talk about hunting for women and how we would avoid settling down with a woman at all cost, but all that changed after I got married. I was singing a new tune and my uncle hadn't gotten to the page of that tune. He was still in his forties and enjoying his bachelor life as if he was George Clooney. Though his investment firm took a hit due to the bad economic times, he somehow managed to keep his head above water and continued to thrive.

Always the sharp dresser, I could see him through the glass sitting behind his desk wearing a sharp, dark grey suit, black shoes, light blue shirt and a nice tie to match. His suit jacket was hanging on the special suit rack located in the corner of his office. My uncle's office was specially designed in a way that afforded him the ability to see his whole staff without stepping out of his office. His business was about hustling all day and he wanted to make sure every single one of those investment bankers he hired stayed busy until they got off the clock. He was driven and he hired the most talented driven folks out of college. My uncle hated failure. I knew which way to walk to keep him from seeing me as I went toward his office. His assistant started to pick up her phone to alert him, but I quickly placed a finger over my mouth signaling to her to keep my presence quiet. Some of the new employees had no idea who I was, so they were staring at me with bewilderment in their eyes. They were wondering who this casual looking dude was that had the authority to walk into the boss's office. The minute I reached for his door he moved away from his computer to catch me right before I stepped into his office. "Nephew!" he screamed as he got up from behind his desk to come around to hug me. "Uncle Joe, how've you been doing? You're looking good as always," I said to him. "You don't look too shabby yourself. How's the family?" he asked. "The family is well. It's been a while since I've seen you, I figured I'd stop by," I told him. "You're still my favorite nephew and you're welcome to stop by anytime," he reassured me. My uncle wasn't the type of man to allow something negative that was bothering him to linger. We had talked my decision to get married and we moved on from there.

Uncle Joe was always my guidance in life and if I ever needed guidance, this was the time. One of the reasons I stopped by his office was because I was looking for options. I needed to find out more than one way to deal with Kendra. My uncle was a logical thinker and problem solver by nature. He could solve anything. I figured I could benefit from his wisdom and point of view. I knew I needed to be rational with my thinking with the Kendra situation. I also needed an objective view as mine was subjective and I didn't want to make a rash decision to end up ruining everything that I was trying to build. "Uncle Joe, I have a serious problem that I'm going to need your help with," I said out of the blue. "How much you need? I'll just write the check. I know you're good for it," he said as he tried to pull his check book out of the draw from his desk. "Nah, it's not any financial problem. My company is doing well enough. I don't need money. I need your wisdom as I always did whenever I had a problem. I have a situation that I think can potentially ruin me if I don't handle it properly," I told him. "It sounds like we need to talk in private about this. Let's into the conference room," he suggested as he grabbed a notepad for notes. My uncle was that meticulous about his problem solving. I don't if that's how he was taught at Harvard Business School, but he wanted to hear the whole story and took notes while he listened.

As I set foot into the conference room I breathed a sigh of relief after my uncle closed the door behind us. I really was struggling with the story, so my uncle suggested that I started from the very beginning. I took his advice and started from the very first time I met Kendra and brought him up to speed to her getting involved with Kevin to get to me. "Junior, you were a target from the very beginning. This woman had you pegged as her prize from the very first day she came to your signing. It was no accident that you ended up having drinks with her, she was sure that would happen. Despite the fact that you're married, you're still a man. And men will always do dumb shit when it comes to beautiful women. Why do you think I've never gotten married? That's because I know I will still do stupid shit when it comes to beautiful women. There's no exception to that rule. You can be a well loved athlete, television personality, reverend, and even the president; you will still act a fool for a beautiful woman. Most men won't admit to their shortcomings because they want to be held in high regards by society, but we all have the same weakness. Having said that, we have to find a solution to your problem," he said.

Now I was excited and anxious to hear what kind of solutions Uncle Joe was going to present to me. I suddenly didn't feel as bad anymore about cheating on my wife. I knew it was wrong, but I believed it was part of a man's nature. It wasn't like I was the first man who ever did it. Bill Clinton got a blowjob from Monica Lewinski while he was sitting in the oval office. Reverend Jesse Jackson was preaching high standards for civil rights while getting his rocks off without even protecting his wife and ended with a child. Bill Cosby was always advocating high morals while he had a concubine for many years. These were all dignified men who had faltered. I never asked anybody to hold me to such high regards.

"Junior, what's done is already done and there's nothing that you can do change it, but this woman is on a destructive path to destroy the very life that you have created until she gets what she wants, which is you. It's delusional, but people like that don't use the same rationale as you and I. You're gonna have to be very careful when dealing with her and you're gonna need a well-executed plan to come out of this unscathed. Now I'm not trying to judge you, but how the hell could you be so stupid and not use a condom while fucking this woman?' my uncle asked in a raised voice. His voice went up a few octaves and I could see the lines on his forehead, denoting his disappointment with me. "I guess I got caught up in the moment and I wanted her to believe that I was gonna leave my wife for her. However, I didn't come in her. I pulled out," I assured him. "Pulling your dick out of some strange woman doesn't shield you from diseases. Based on what you've told me about this woman, she could be walking around carrying a number of diseases. You need to go have yourself checked before you try to get intimate with your wife," he emphatically proposed. "As a matter of fact, I'll go to the clinic after I leave here," I promised him. "Junior, I'm afraid this lady is going try to pin you up against Kevin in order to bring you down as well. She has too much information on you," he said. I was starting to feel hopeless as my uncle went on and on about how this woman had me in the palm of her hands. He did this to show me the negative side of the situation, but my uncle was never the type of man to go into anything without weighing both sides. I felt a sense of relief as he shifted position and started telling what we were going to do to get rid of Kendra without it affecting my livelihood and family life.

I astutely sat there and listened to my uncle as he went over his plan with me to get rid of Kendra. I was as excited as a little kid the night before Christmas. My uncle was a genius, I thought. My uncle was concerned about me walking around Boston carrying a loaded gun, which I didn't have a license for. The statute for carrying a concealed loaded weapon in Boston is an automatic five years in the State prison. He wanted to keep me from jail. He suggested that I returned the gun to Kevin immediately. He also told me that Kendra was going to drag Kevin along for as long as she could until she figured out a way to use him to her advantage. Kevin was not going to get ass from her any time soon, if at all. Her target was me and that was all she cared about. After leaving his office, I was a lot more optimistic about getting rid of Kendra. I couldn't wait to start implementing the plan. But first, I had to go to the clinic to get checked out for some venereal diseases.

Dirty Game

I received a clean bill of health from the clinic. The only results that I couldn't get right away were the HIV test results. I had to wait a few weeks to get those. Meanwhile, I felt a little better that I wasn't walking around with Chlamydia, gonorrhea or syphilis. I couldn't use my regular clinic for these tests, so I went to Roxbury in order to keep from getting busted by my wife. I had to pay cash for everything, and that shit wasn't cheap. I got out of the clinic so late I completely forgot to call Kevin to get the gun back to him. By the time I made it back home, I needed to get ready to go meet with Kendra. I took a quick shower when I got home and kissed all my babies and my wife goodbye a few minutes later. I didn't want my wife to ask too many questions, so I told her I had to go to a business meeting in Boston and that I would be back shortly. I wore basic black; black slack, black shoes, black shirt, a black jacket and a black hat. The one thing that I loved about my wife was that she never interfered with my business. She knew what I needed to do to pay the bills and she never got in the way of it.

I showed up on Park and Boylston Street at exactly 8:00 PM as scheduled. It's usually not that hard to find a parking space after business hours downtown, but that particular day, I wasn't so lucky. I didn't want to leave any trace of Kendra in my car, so I tried my best to avoid having her in it. Just as she was walking toward me to get in the car, I noticed this guy pulling out of a parking space. I quickly put the car in drive and I maneuvered my way into the space in less than thirty seconds. I was relieved to do it because only Lord knows what kind of sneaky stunt Kendra would've pulled to leave evidence in my car for my wife to find. I jumped out of the car and walked toward her. I hugged her as if nothing was wrong. She wanted to hold me a little longer, but I pointed toward the Boston Common and suggested we take a walk through there.

Kendra was all smiles as we walked through the park hand-in-hand like two young love birds. I had initially planned on confronting Kendra with the gun, but my plans changed after meeting with my uncle. I needed to revert back to my Casanova ways in order to rid myself of this headache of a woman. "I wanted to meet you here to ask you to be patient with me, because I realize that your heart belongs to me and you are truly the woman that I should be with. I wanna love you for the rest of my life, but I can't jeopardize the welfare of my children. I can't just up and walk out of their lives," I told her with my best Oscar performance yet. "I know baby. I didn't mean to do all the things I did to you. It drives me crazy knowing that you're sleeping with that woman every night. She's not even good enough for you. She's going to cheat on you just like she cheated on her first husband. I would never do that to you," she revealed. I really could've reached back and slapped the mention of my wife out of her mouth, but I chilled. I was there to convince her that we would be together and I wanted to make sure that was done.

"I'm feeling a little hungry, do you wanna grab a bite to eat?" she asked. "Not really. I just wanna be in your arms and spend every moment with you. We should go back to your room and order room service," I said. Kendra's eyes lit up. She immediately turned around and started walking across the park to her hotel at the Park Plaza. I had the biggest phony smile on my face as I started telling Kendra I couldn't wait to rip her clothes off and make love to her all night. "I'm getting moist just thinking about you fucking the hell outta me," she whispered in my ear while flashing a big Kool Aid smile. I was already in hot water. I needed to find a way to cool down the temperature. After we made it to the room, Kendra sat me down and started unzipping my pants to take my dick in her mouth. I decided to play it like a scene out of Harlem Nights. As Kendra started sucking my dick, I picked up the phone to call my wife to tell her I wanted a divorce, but little did Kendra know, I had already pressed the recording button on my cell phone and she was now on candid camera sucking my dick. The only image that was seen was her slobbing on a big dick. It could've been any man. I never pulled my pants down. She unzipped my pants, pulled my dick out and started sucking the skin off it. I had some of the best footage, but a few minutes later, I would even better footage when I decided to lift her skirt and fuck her from behind after wrapping myself in a condom. No part of my body was ever exposed on camera. The only thing that was seen was my penis going in and out her pussy and the expression on her face as she screamed, "Give it to me, daddy. Your dick is so good." I was very happy with my performance, and by the end of the night, I had Kendra believe that we were going to be a couple very soon.

While I was at the hotel with Kendra, I found out she was only in town for one more day. She had to return back to her real job as a lawyer in order to continue to maintain the lifestyle that afforded her the opportunity to stalk me around the country. I also asked Kendra what she was going to do about Kevin, and she told me not to worry about it. "I don't want that street thug. What can a man like that do for me? I'm trying to get married and have a family with a professional man, not some two-bit hustler who thinks the streets are paved with gold. Kevin is irrelevant," she said while I still had my camera rolling. I suspected she knew she had Kevin wrapped around her fingers and she was going to dispose of him because she felt she no longer needed him to force my decision to be with her. I left Kendra feeling confident that I had the situation under control. I knew I had to get out of there because Kevin had mentioned he was supposed to see her later that night.

The Beat Goes On

Kendra may have been acting a certain way with Kevin when she was at my house, but Kevin was more than happy to divulge information to me about his relationship with Kendra. According to Kevin, Kendra was a freak who liked to be licked in every way. Though he hadn't yet gotten to fuck her, but it was in his future plans. Kevin was also falling for Kendra. Not so much for the real person that Kendra was, but for whom she fabricated herself to be. Holding back information about her from him was the most difficult thing to do because I had never seen such passion coming from him when he talked about a woman. Kevin was one of those guys who didn't get attached to women because there was always an abundance of them available to him. Even though most of them fell in the hoodrat category, there was still an abundance of them. He thought Kendra, or should I say Kandy, was the classiest woman he had ever met. Kendra was skillful at making herself look good, but the way Kevin was falling so fast could place her life in jeopardy.

I had to do a little research of my own after Kevin revealed Kendra's new alias to me. I talked her into telling me the name of the firm that she worked for in Miami so I could check her out. I did call the firm and they verified that Kendra was indeed one of the associates at the law firm, but she was supposed to be doing research in Atlanta on a case assigned to her by her boss. They told me that she was out of the office for a month and she would return soon. Kendra was well-paid and her talent was highly respected by her peers. However, I sensed some discomfort from the woman that I talked to when I called the firm. I had positioned myself as a power player seeking representation by the firm through a referral. I specifically wanted Kendra to represent me, but I wanted a little history on her. Without saying so bluntly, the woman made Kendra sound like a woman scorned because she had lost her husband to another woman at the firm. The woman had since left the firm and married Kendra's ex-husband. Since then, Kendra had left no prisoners and had been on a path to destroy as many marriages as possible, according to the woman I talked to.

I was starting to get a clearer picture of Kendra by the day. I started to wonder why she chose me. Then I thought about the plot in my last book that resembled her real life. This woman didn't want to be with me. She was out to destroy me. She was known as a man eater. Because her man had left her for another woman, she started to believe that all men were cheaters and she was out get them one by one. I was easy to get because my life was an open book, thanks to *The Bedroom Bandit*, my first book. This woman was just as much a pretender as I was. I started thinking about poor Kevin. The one thing that Kevin hated the most was women who slept around. He often talked about what he would if his woman ever cheated on him. Most of his tales were torturous. One of the reasons he remained by himself was because he thought very little of the women he encountered. He felt there was a price tag attached to every woman. Kendra was the first woman he met that he didn't feel that way about. He respected her for some reason. I have to believe that Kendra's beauty, more than her accomplishment, was the reason that Kevin was head- over-heels for her.

When I got home, I went directly to my office and shut the door. My kids were already sleeping and my wife was in the bedroom on her way to sleep as well. I wanted to download the video of Kendra sucking me and me fucking her onto a disc. I needed to get that image off my phone because my kids sometimes played it and I didn't want them to be traumatized by those vulgar images. After downloading the image to a disk, I also made another copy onto my travel drive. I knew for sure that I was going to get rid of Kendra once and for all. There was no way she was going to keep on after I sent my little video to her.

Crazy In Love

Meanwhile, something weird was taking place in Kevin's heart. He was falling in love. I don't know if he was so used to women giving up the drawers so quickly to him, but he had a higher level of respect for Kendra because she didn't. Kendra was a great people reader and manipulator and I was sure she figured out a way to manipulate Kevin by holding out on him, or if she even planned on sleeping with him at all. Kevin called me early the next morning to tell me how he spent the night with Kendra and made her cum over and over while eating her and that was satisfying to him. His thug ass never even talked about eating pussy, but now he was an expert. "Yo Dave, she told me she was falling in love with me and she didn't want to give herself to me too soon because I was special to her," he said. I was thinking to myself, *What the hell kind of thug are you? Can't you see through this woman?* I guess Kevin was blinded and I didn't have the right prescription to correct his vision. "Like I told you before, man, take your time and make sure this is what you wanna do before jumping in with both feet," I cautioned. "I understand what you're saying. She invited

- 177 -

me to come down to Miami with her. She wants me to stay at her house with her, too," he said sounding happier than a lottery winner. I was a little shock that Kendra would invite Kevin to her house after what she told me about him. Now I was thrown for a loop and I really needed to be careful with her. "So when are you leaving?" I asked with curiosity. "I'm catching the last flight out. She left this morning," he informed me. I almost slipped up and said, "I know."

Now I was more confused than ever. I wondered what the hell Kendra wanted from me. The day had just begun for me and I started out on the wrong foot so early in the morning. I wanted to call Kendra to see what was up, but her phone was off because she was on the plane. By this time, I had started to tune out Kevin because my mind was running a thousand miles a minute trying to figure out Kendra's motive and next course of action. However, he was completely unaware of my action toward him. He was dishing out his plan on how he was going to make Kendra his wife and trying to stay focused on his writing so he could give up the street hustling. 'I thought you told me you already gave that up," I said to him. I may not have been listening, but I heard the pertinent information and needed to address it. "Man, don't even start with the third degree. You know I ain't been making the kind of money to be driving the kind of car I'm driving. I can live that lifestyle now because people assume my shit is legit, but you and I both know the real deal. I gotta ball, Dave," he said to me. "You're a grown-ass man, so you should know what's good for you. Maybe it's a good thing that Kendra, I mean Kandy, came into your life. You need to give up that slinging game," I said sternly to him. He paused for a minute before he came back and said, "Man, you know how many drug dealers think they can walk away from this shit after making the money they want to make? If it was that easy, we'd have a bunch of rich retired mo'fucking drug dealers chilling in South Beach. The paper I make from my book ain't even a tenth of what I make on the street. All these people who I look-out for don't care how I make my money. They all think that I'm a successful author, including my mother. What am I supposed to let her think that I can't take care of her anymore? I can't do that. I got one last big run to make before I leave this shit alone, and then I can focus on my writing," he said. All I could think was that he was going to be writing the rest of his books in prison for continuing to fool himself. Kevin's analogy made no sense to me. I couldn't understand why most drug dealers feel they need to pull one last deal before walking away. That last deal is always the reason they end up behind bars or dead. I really didn't know what to say to Kevin. I stayed silent on the phone for about a minute before he came back and said, "Yo, I gotta get going. I'll holla at you later, one."

After hanging up the phone with Kevin, I realized that everything he was doing was really for other people and not himself. He needed to make other people believe in him. I guess that was his way of validating himself. I always thought he was bright and knew what he wanted out of life, but after that conversation I realized Kevin was a statistic waiting to happen. He was no different than many other young black men who fell in love with the allure of the street. The absence of a male role model in his life contributed greatly to his perspective and his search for acceptance from other people. Like Kevin, I grew up with a single mother, but uncle stepped in and assumed the responsibility of not only a father, but also as a role model in my life. I never took the time to really talk to my friend, but I was feeling like I'd failed him. All these issues were mounting and I felt that something tragic was going to come out of the situation. I wondered what Kevin was really in love with, Kendra or the lifestyle he had people believe he was living?

The Battle Within

While Kevin was gone to Miami, I was conflicted about two things. The first issue was the fact that I thought Kevin was on destructive path and needed to be saved. And the second issue was the possibility of losing my family because of this crazy-ass chick. I wanted to pick and choose, but I couldn't. They were both worthy causes, and both important to me. Kevin wasn't just a friend to me, he had become a brother. All those years we spent together as friends when we were kids, it never dawned on me that Kevin was missing out on so much. I needed to save my marriage, but I also needed to save my friend. I knew it was none of my business to interfere in his life, but I cared too much about him to sit on the sideline and watch. Coming up with a plan to get Kevin out of the game wasn't going to be easy, but it had to be done. I wanted so much to talk to my wife about the pressure that Kevin was under, but I felt like I was betraying his trust by doing that.

I only knew one person that could help me come up with a solution, and it was my uncle. Kevin was like a nephew to him too; he watched us grow up together. Most of the time, my uncle would take myself, Kevin and Rammel out to the park to play ball. He was very familiar with my friends, as I only had two. At one point, he became overly concerned with Kevin because he had seen them dealing on the block a couple of times. My uncle knew that he didn't need to talk to me about being negatively influenced by Kevin. He had done a great job helping to rear me. I needed his help to keep Kevin from self-destruction.

It was October and playoff season for Major League Baseball. As a fan of the Red Sox, I knew my uncle wouldn't up the opportunity to go to one of their playoff games. I did some wheeling and dealing and I was able to land two tickets to watch the Red Sox play the Cleveland Indians. I didn't even have to ask Uncle Joe twice, he was more than happy to go to the game with me. I knew that the game would give us the opportunity to talk and I desperately needed to talk to him about the latest revelation with my situation, as well as saving Kevin from the streets.

I picked up Uncle Joe from his house and we made it to Fenway Park just in time for the game to start. It was a sold out crowd and we had decent seats. Red Sox fans can be obnoxious, but we were right along with them rooting for the home team. While watching the game, I began to update my Uncle about my situation with Kendra and he was surprised with the turn of events. A new plan had to be devised because we didn't know where Kendra was going to take her shenanigans. After talking about Kendra and establishing a new plan to deal with her, we moved on to Kevin, his involvement with the street and Kendra. My uncle assured me he would assist to help prevent Kevin from being swallowed by the streets. Kendra, however, we had to wait and see. There were many plans in place depending on which direction she wanted to take it.

Satisfied with what my uncle told me with pen and pencil as he usually did, we turned to the game and started yelling at the top our lungs for the Sox to beat the Indians. We had drunk white people all around us. They were trying to high-five each other after each hit and would miss as if their rhythm-less butts were on a dance floor. My uncle and I were cracking up as these white people were trying their best to make the only two Negroes in our section feel comfortable. It was funny how they tried to change their vernacular to relate to us as if we couldn't understand proper English. Each time one of them tried to brush up on his ebonics, my uncle responded in the whitest tone that he could put together to make them feel as stupid as they sounded. We laughed our asses off on our way home talking about how the drunken white boys felt we were so different from them. Shit like that could only happen in Boston.

Family Time

I had been so consumed with Kendra that I completely shut my family out. I needed to spend some quality time with them and Saturday was one of the better days to do something as a family. I got up early and made breakfast for everyone. My wife and kids sat at the table with me and we ate pancakes, bacon, eggs and toast. Savant kept praising my efforts while my wife held in her laugh. She couldn't believe the affection and appreciation my kids were showing me for cooking for them. Daniella kept saying, "Mommy's food is good too." I couldn't agree more. The kids had gotten so used to watching their mom cook, it was abnormal to see daddy in the kitchen. After breakfast, I helped my wife get the kids ready for our events of the day. It was fun to finally do something as a family. I was to blame for the lack of involvement with my family because I was always working. I needed to change even if it was just for one day.

The fall season in New England is one of the most beautiful seasons, and there is always so much to do. I decided to pack the family in the truck to go apple picking in western Massachusetts in a little town called Whately at Quonquont Farm. Because Rammell went to school in Western Massachusetts at Williams College, I was familiar with Quonquont Farm and the surrounding areas. Rammell, Kevin and I went to Quonquont Farm once with a group of young ladies from Williams College while we visited Rammel at school. We were trying to find something different to do. It ended up being a lot of fun. We ate so much fruit that weekend we almost got sick. After loading up the truck, we hit the road with the children's favorite DVDs so they could have something to do on the two hour drive to Whately. My wife and I reconnected while the kids enjoyed their favorite show on the DVD player mounted in the on the back of the two front seats in my Mercedes 450 GL truck. When they got bored with the shows, we did some sing along. We brought snacks and water for the children in case they got hungry. My daughters love apples and oranges, so my wife peeled a couple and placed them in ziplock sandwich bags for them. All Joseph cared about was his bottle. We brought a couple of bottles for him and diapers in case he decided to have a moment. It was a lot of fun on the way up there. I held my wife's hand most of the way up.

It had been almost two hours and I was excited and announced, "We're almost there," to the family when I saw the sign for exit 24 to Deerfield off I-91 South. I knew that we were close and I didn't want the two girls to start falling asleep. Joseph was long gone and would have to be woken up anyway. My little man fell asleep the minute I shifted the car into drive. The farm opened from 10:00AM to 6:00PM. Since we got there around noon, we had plenty of time to go apples, blueberries, peaches and raspberries picking. The girls were excited. They had never been to a farm before. Quonquont Farm offered a variety of natural habitats. The apple and peach orchards were just the tip of the iceberg. They had several acres of hay meadow, a spring-fed farm pond to house frogs, salamanders, dragonflies, fish and turtles. It also encompassed what's called the Whately "Dingle"- a lovely valley of flowers and ferns intersected by a small brook. The farm's hemlock and hickory woodlands also extended back to Bull Mountain and the Conway State Forest. As a family, we had plenty to do for the next six hours and we did it all until we were tired. While there, we also learned the history of the farm and its name, which originated from a 17th century Native American leader who lived nearby along the Connecticut River. My daughter was fascinated and kept asking questions about the different sites. It was a day well spent and a day to remember for the whole family.

From the smirk on my wife's face on the drive back home from the farm, I knew she was happy that I dedicated a day to the family. Of course our day didn't end there. After unloading the truck and bringing the fruit back in the house we got back in the car and went to my kids' favorite Chinese restaurant, Cathay Pacific, in Neponset for dinner. It was almost 8:00PM when we got to the restaurant. Since we were already au courant of the restaurant's dishes, there was no need to look at a menu. We ordered our usual Pu Pu platter consisting of egg rolls, skewered teriyaki steak, tempura shrimp, fried wontons, fried ribs, and chicken fingers. We also ordered a side of fried rice. We feasted on the food until our bellies were full. By the time we left the restaurant, they were about to close. On the short drive home from the restaurant, all the kids fell asleep. When we got home all we had to do was put them to bed. My wife and I tried our best to stay to see if we could sneak a quickie while the kids were sleeping, but we were too tired to follow through with it. We fell asleep, too.

Back To The Situation

A week went by and I didn't hear from Kevin or Kendra. My mother always said, "No news is good news." I was happy not to hear from either of them. As a matter of fact, I was finally able to get some sleep. I was hoping the two of them fell in love and she would forget that I ever existed. It was only a wish and no sooner was I thinking that, that she called. It was a good thing I was in the car driving down to the South End to go pick up the new bookmarks that I had ordered for Kevin's new book. "What's going on?" I casually said through the receiver after I noticed Kendra's number. "I was dealing with a situation down here, I couldn't call you for a few days," she said as if I cared. "Don't worry about it. Take care of your business. I'm good," I said in a callous way, hoping she would get the hint. "Dave, you still haven't told me the official date that you're going to separate from your wife. I know a divorce can take a while, but there's no reason for you to continue to live in the same house as her," she said matter-of-factly. This chick had the nerve to tell me what to do. "Where do you suppose I live?" I asked with sarcasm in my voice. "If it was up to me, you'd be living down here with me," she said. I had the best come back yet and I couldn't wait to let it roll off my tongue and sting her ears. "If I move in with you, where's Kevin going to sleep? Aren't you guys a couple?" I said while holding in my laugh. "You must think this is a joke. I don't have time for games, David. You better tell your wife you're leaving or I'm going to come up there and do it for you. I'm sure she will be more than happy to watch her husband fuck the hell out of me on tape," she said in a cocky way.

Up to this point, I really wished Kendra would go away on her own, but since she didn't seem to want to do that, I had decided to help her. "Have you checked your email lately?" I asked with a smirk in my voice. "No. Why?" she asked. "Well, since you like to make threats, I decided to show you that I can be just as threatening. I believe actions speak louder than words. If you don't leave me the hell alone, every single person in your office will find the same email in their inbox in a couple of days. I suggest you watch what you say to me and I don't want to hear any more threats coming from you," I said with confidence before I continued, "One more thing, don't fucking call my number again or I will fucking ruin you!" I hung up the phone before she had a chance to respond.

My uncle and I had been planning this coup against Kendra, and everything seemed to have been working just the way we planned it. Now, it was Kendra's move and she had better proceed with caution. The reason I was able to talk so forcefully with Kendra was because I received a text from my uncle saying, "It's done." I knew exactly what the text meant and I couldn't wait to see if Kendra would have the gall to call me and trying to proceed with her bullshit. Based on the reaction I'd receive from her, I would go a different route if I had to. I was driving and keeping my fingers crossed that we had done enough damage to repeal her. Kendra knew she could destroy my marriage, but she couldn't destroy my professional life, whereas in her case, things were completely different. I couldn't believe she was trying to go up against an army with a handgun. I had something for that ass that would put her ass back in her place.

Just as I was smiling and feeling relieved that I had gotten rid of Kendra for good, I received another call from her. "Motherfucker, you think I give a fuck about an email showing me sucking your dick!? I don't give a shit about that. These people at my job don't mean shit to me. Besides, I can sue your ass because I never gave you permission to videotape me," she said angrily. Since she had brought up the fact that I didn't have permission to videotape her, I decided to use her own argument against her. "I guess you thought you had the right to videotape me, huh? I will sue your ass too if you don't get rid of that tape. I don't want your ass and I don't care about your ass. You better leave me the fuck alone before this goes somewhere you don't want it to go," I said before slamming the phone down in her ear. My uncle was the culprit behind me videotaping Kendra. He figured if we threatened to send it to her law firm, she would back down, but this crazy loon didn't give a damn. I guessed we were going to have to move to plan B.

Just as I was picking up the phone to call my uncle to inform him she didn't bite, Kendra called me again. I needed to talk to her to figure out her state of mind and next move. "Let me tell you something, I'm the last bitch you ever think you're just gonna fuck and walk away from. I'm tired of you tired-ass men thinking that you can have shit your way all the time. You wanna send your little video to my firm? Go right ahead, but when my gavel comes down, it's going to come down harder," she threatened before hanging up on me this time. Kendra seemed like she was beyond scorned and I really needed to watch my next move. I frantically picked up the phone and called my uncle. Now I was second-guessing whether or not plan B was a strong enough plan to get rid of Kendra. My uncle had to help me calm down through the phone because I felt like I was losing my grip on the situation.

Playing The Fool

Kevin came back home from Miami feeling like he was on top of the world. I was the first person he called on his way home from the airport. "Yo Dave, I think she's the one, dawg. I'm about to go to the store to get her a ring to wrap things up," he said. I knew he was talking about Kendra, but I had to play dumb. "Who you talking about, Kev?" I said acting like I had forgotten about Kendra or Kandy or whatever the hell she called herself. "I'm talking about Kandy, man. The pussy was the bomb and I got the best head that I had ever gotten in my life from her," he said. I started thinking that maybe Kevin had never really gotten a good blowjob from the chickenheads he was screwing. I had yet to meet a woman that could suck my dick like my wife, and that was with Kendra included. Hell, Kendra's performance didn't even come close to my wife's. I was sitting there on the phone and thinking about how this fool was ready to go out and buy a ring because of a fucking blowjob.

"So you think you're ready to marry this woman because you felt her pussy was the bomb and her head game was off the charts? What about all the other components that make a relationship work? Do they even matter to you?" I asked curiously. "Yo, the chick is a motherfucking doctor, she got paper and she fine as hell. I ain't got nothing to worry about," he said. This fool had no idea that Kendra was lying to him. I wanted so much to burst his bubble, but I didn't want to be the one to crush him. I learned a very long time ago that no one should ever have the need to tell someone negative information about a love interest. It would only lead to the destruction of the friendship because the heart tends to get attached blindly and most of us lose our logical sense when it comes to love, especially in the beginning.

The detriment to Kevin's livelihood was becoming secondary by the day. I had to devise a plan for him to see the truth in Kendra. "Yo Kev, where you at right now?" I asked. "I'm heading down to Copley as we speak so I can get a ring for Kandy. You think fifteen grand is enough for a nice ring? I like Marsha's ring. How much did that set you back?" he asked. There were so many questions, I didn't know which one deserved a response, or if any of them deserved a response at all. "Kev, can we talk about this before you make any rash decisions? Can we meet right quick? I got a few things that I think we should talk about before you take this leap. After all, I am the married one here and I have more experience with this sort of thing than you do," I said trying to use a more philosophical approach. "Why don't you come to the mall to meet me, I should be there in about a half," he said. Thirty minutes wasn't going to cut it for me. I had a few loose ends to tie up with my uncle before I would be able to meet with Kevin. I just wished that fool would just wait to talk to me before he went and spent too much money on a ring for a woman who wasn't worth it. "I can't get there in a half hour, but I can make in forty five minutes to an hour. Is that good?" I asked. "Man, just hurry your ass on down here. If you don't get here soon, I'mma go ahead and pick the ring out myself," he said. I didn't know why he thought I was coming down to support his decision to buy a ring, but whatever.

As soon as I got off the phone with Kevin, I called my uncle to tell him about Kevin's plan and how we needed to make a move fast with our plan B. Time was not on our side, but it was worse when I checked my watch and noticed that an hour had already gone by while My uncle and I discussed plan B to get rid of Kendra. I had to hurry down to Copley to go meet with Kevin. The drive from my house to Copley would be an additional half hour, but knowing Kevin, I figured he would go walk around the mall for a little while because he was addicted to shopping.

The Salacious Dreamer

All I could hope for was that Kevin didn't already purchase the ring before I got to him. It would be hard to pry fifteen grand back from one of those jewelers in Copley. Kevin also had a bad habit of keeping a lot of money in a special compartment in his car. He always felt that he could be arrested at any time. He thought the money could bring him liberty and peace of mind if he ever got locked up. My race against time engulfed my mind and I started thinking about the worse possible situation for Kevin. My mind was wandering and I couldn't help but imagine myself walking into Kevin's house to find him gone and his wife taking me upstairs to give me a taste of her goodies because she felt she married the wrong man.

"You know you're the reason I married Kevin. I wanted you and you didn't want me, but my heart still aches for you," I imagined Kendra telling me as she grabbed my hand to bring them between her breasts so I could feel the rhythm of her heartbeat. She slowly pushed my hands toward her breasts so I could get a feel of her erected nipples. "No man has ever made love to me the way you have, Dave, not even Kevin," she said. My ego was enjoying my imagination a little too much, but I still didn't wake up from my daydream. "How about you take me upstairs and make me squirm once more for old time sake," she said, while opening the silk robe she was wearing to exposed her shaven pussy and her perky breasts to me. The excitement of sleeping with another man's woman in his own house took over my senses. I allowed Kendra to lead me up the stairs to the master bedroom. The thought of Kevin walking through the house at any moment to catch me in the act never even crossed my mind.

Kendra's skin was a lot more supple, and her body reeked of this sweet smelling perfume that I couldn't make out, nor did I care. I ran my hands through her flowing locks as we locked lip while I sat on the edge of the bed and she stood between my legs. My hands ran circles around her shoulders after she disrobed. The anticipation of her perky breasts in my mouth could last no longer as I took one nipple and started to suckle on it like I had been deprived for years. "Mmmm, baby," she moaned as my tongued worked its magic on her nipple. The moaning sound of her voice fueled the demon in my pants as it started to suck all the blood flow from my heart. I was nine and a half inches hard and Kendra could feel it near her gut as we stood holding each other with our tongues tied in passion. At first, a little groping of my dick seemed to have been sufficed, but as the passion between us started to heat up, Kendra couldn't help herself. She wanted to taste me. She slowly made her way down and unfastened my belt and pants to take my sweet dick in her mouth for a flavorful mouth-bursting sensational experience. The twirling of her tongue around my shaft had my body convulsing like I was having a heart attack.

As she knelt between my legs with my dick in her mouth, all I could think about was filling up her pussy with my overgrown dick. I pulled her up, turned her towards the bed and bent her over so I could penetrate her from behind. I hadn't really paid much attention when I came to the house, but as Kendra spread open her legs, I could see the sexy silhouette of her pussy better because of the five inch heels she was wearing. My first thought was to just take my dick and rub it over her clit to get her moist enough to penetrate her. However, the contour of her pussy looked so good I decided to have her sit on my chest while I devoured her pussy with my tongue. I couldn't help wanting to eat a beautiful pussy. I don't know how I was able to focus on the road while daydreaming about fucking Kendra, but I did it, somehow. I spread her pussy lips open as my tongue made its way inside, tasting her sweet juices while my fingers rubbed on her pulsating clit. "Oh shit," she started mumbling while winding on my face. "You eat my pussy so well. Oh shit, I'm cumming. Ahhhhhhhh!" she screamed as she came. It was then that I realized that I had reached my destination and I needed to refocus so my dick could go down.

I thought I'd reached Kevin just in time, but I was a little too late when I saw the black bag in his hand with the jewelry store name boldly written on it in silver. I was disappointed that I got there so late, but Kevin was the happiest that I had ever seen him. "Yo Dave, I went all out for shawty. Check this out," he said as he opened the box to reveal a four carat diamond ring. The ring was breathtaking and beautiful and no way in hell did Kendra deserve it. "That's a nice ring, Kev. What, you spent your whole life savings on it?" I asked sarcastically. "Nah. I just want her to know that I can handle a woman like her and I'm gonna do whatever it takes to make her happy. I got the ring for twenty-five Gs," he revealed. I had no idea Kevin was driving around with that kind of money in his car. "Yo, I know you don't keep that kind of money in your car all the time, right?" I asked curiously. "Not that much all the time, but I do keep cash in the ride. Dealing with these crackheads and drug addicts all the time, sometime they have good deals and I want to have the money to buy the shit from them," he said. Here I was thinking he kept the money in the car in case he got locked up. He continued, "I didn't have time to put the money in the safe before I went to Miami, so I left it in the car at the airport," he said nonchalantly.

I couldn't believe that Kevin went out and spent so much on a ring for a woman he barely knew. What could have taken place that blurred his vision so quickly? I wondered. Well, I didn't have to wonder too long because Kevin was more than happy to divulge the details of his sexual romps with Kendra while he was in Florida. "Yo Dave, she got the best body I have ever seen period. My dick stayed hard the whole week while I was with her. We ended up staying in a hotel in South Beach because she was getting some work done to her house," he told me. I started to think about the manipulation that Kevin had just experienced at the hands of Kendra and I realized I needed to be a lot more careful with her. "So, did you ever confirm that she was a doctor?" I enquired. "Man, shawty got up everyday and went to work at the hospital. She had one of those white jackets that the doctors ear with a name tag and a stethoscope that she brought to the hotel with her. I don't think she's lying about that," he said convincingly. I guessed Kendra went all out to convince Kevin she was a doctor. I needed to do my own research about her being an attorney.

I hated to pretend, but I didn't want Kevin to feel that I was envious of him in any way whatsoever, so I decided to congratulate him on his future engagement and wished him luck with his new psycho, I mean girlfriend. The damage was already done so there was no changing Kevin's mind about Kendra. I decided to leave it alone in order to save face and maintain my relationship with Kevin as well as his sister who was my wife. Before I walked away, I handed the gun back to Kevin and thanked him for letting me borrow it.

A Shocking Discovery

After talking to Kendra, she didn't seem fazed by my threats and she was pushing me even more to tell my wife I wanted to leave her. I knew another approach would be better suited not only for me, but for my family. It wasn't unusual for Kevin to receive fan mail at the office. Tons of prisoners who read his book sent letters to congratulate him on a well-written book. It wasn't often, but he also received letters from everyday normal readers as well. Before Kevin traveled anywhere, he always stopped by the office to get a list of available bookstores in the area where he's traveling so he could do some book signings. He always waited until the last minute to pick up the schedule from the receptionist, but on this particular day, there was also a package waiting for him at the office. Since he didn't do any book-signings the last time he visited Florida because he thought he was going to be spending most of his time with Kendra, he decided he would busy this time by doing signings while she was at work. His book-signing schedule was handed to him along with the package that arrived without a returned address. He placed them in his laptop case.

Kevin also traveled with his laptop wherever he went because the ideas for his books were always flowing around in his head. As planned Kevin drove himself to the airport to get on his fight so he could go ask Kendra her hand in marriage. While Kevin was in the air anticipating a love-fest reunion with Kendra, I decided to do some digging of my own. A little investigation could go a long way. I couldn't simply rely on a plan that my uncle and I had put together. I had to know who my adversary was and how I needed to deal with her.

A quick search on Google for the name Kendra Phillips revealed a very accomplished young woman from Miami Florida. Kendra Phillips was not only a lawyer, but she also studied plastic surgery in medical school. She graduated from the University of Florida with a dual degree in biology and political science. Soon after college, she enrolled at the University of Miami's Miller School of Medicine where she studied to become a plastic surgeon. After a four year residency at one of the top hospitals in Florida, Kendra decided to start her own practice. Business was booming and Kendra was doing well in Florida as a plastic surgeon. Her clientele consisted mostly of baby boomers that were not ready to let go of their youthful beauty. When Botox was first introduced to the market,

Kendra's list of client quadrupled. She was always busy and she loved the life that working as a plastic surgeon provided for her. Kendra's head was in the clouds as she was raking in millions of dollars every year as one of the best plastic surgeons in South Florida. I was surprised at all the information that I found on Kendra, but I wasn't satisfied. While still researching her background, I also called my uncle to see if he could pull some strings to find out a little more private information for me from one of his friends at FBI headquarters.

Online, I found out Kendra's practice was doing well, but she was consumed by her work. Sometimes she was even too tired to go to work, but she couldn't pass on the money. One day while performing a procedure under duress, she mistakenly injected a client with Botox in the wrong area. A simple procedure she had done thousands of times before. Her mistake resulted in a slight deformity on the client's face. She was sued and had to settle with the client before she lost the shirt on her back. She was angry with her representation, but it was a little too late when the judge slammed his gavel and rendered a verdict in favor of the plaintiff. Just as quickly as she built her reputation as one of the top plastic surgeons in South Florida, her reputation took a nose dive after the verdict was announced in the media. She started losing clients so she closed her practice and went back to work for a local hospital.

Unsatisfied with her job at the hospital, Kendra went back to school to obtain a Jurist Doctorate to practice law. Kendra was determined to become one of the best lawyers in the country. She rose through the ranks at her firm in no time. She had vowed to never become a victim of a lawsuit again. She acknowledged her mistake with the patient, but she was angry at the lack of competence from her attorney. While working as an attorney, Kendra started to reflect on her life. She wanted to find purpose in her life. She decided volunteering her time at a local shelter would bring a different kind of gratification, and it did.

A few years later, Kendra befriended a young woman named Latrice at the homeless shelter where volunteered. The young woman admired everything about Kendra. The admiration soon became mutual as Kendra took on the role of mentor for this young woman. However, the young woman suffered a bad case of low self-esteem. She was always insecure about her looks because she didn't get the attention she felt she deserved from the young men at her school. Kendra became so involved in Latrice's life, she decided to take her in and became the legal guardian for her. Due to the lack of technology back in the 80's, Kendra had no way to confirm the true identity of Latrice other than what Latrice had told her and the paperwork she presented as identification to Kendra. After Latrice moved into Kendra's mansion, she became fascinated with Kendra's life. The glamour, the celebrity friends, the money and the fame made Latrice envious of her mentor.

Though things were going great between Latrice and Kendra, there was still an issue that Latrice needed to work on, and that was her self-esteem and appearance. There was no other person she admired more than Kendra and she told Kendra one day, "I bet if I looked like you, I wouldn't have half the problems that I'm having in my life with the boys." Kendra raised her eyebrows at first because she had no idea where Latrice was headed with her statement, but as weeks passed, Latrice brought the subject up again. This time she suggested that Kendra did an operation that would make her look just like Kendra. At first, Kendra thought the idea was crazy, however, as a surgeon, she had become narcissistic because she felt she was playing god, making people look the way they wanted to look. Not only that, she thought the highest compliment she could receive was to have someone who wanted to look like her and not a famous movie star.

Latrice and Kendra were living like sisters. They were the same complexion and wore the same size in clothing. There was no limit to what Kendra allowed Latrice to do. She gave Latrice access to everything, including her closet, cars, shoes and even her money sometimes. She really treated her like the sister she always wanted to have. "I always wanted to have a twin sister, I guess you looking like will be similar," Kendra said while sipping tea at the kitchen table with Latrice. Soon laughter followed and the two women started joking about the ways they would trick their men if they looked identical. Since Latrice was in college at the time, Kendra thought it was a bad idea to change her look in the middle of her sophomore semester. She suggested that Latrice waited until she graduated from college to get the procedure done. Kendra was an advocate for higher education and she wanted to make sure Latrice made something out of her life.

A victim of the foster care system, Kendra knew what it was like to struggle. Her mother dropped her off at the hospital wrapped in a towel and never returned. She bounced from one foster home to another as a child. By the time she was a teenager, Kendra devised a plan to take control of her life. Though life was hard at the last home where she stayed, Kendra never lost sight of her plan to graduate at the top of her high school so she could attend college. She clearly was able to identify with Latrice, and that was one of the reasons she decided to help Latrice. As time went on Latrice continued to plead with Kendra for a new look. She even told Kendra she wanted to transfer to a different school to get a fresh start. It was at after that suggestion that Kendra decided to perform the procedure for Latrice. It took a few weeks for the recovery process, but when it was over and done, Latrice was a mirror image of Kendra. She couldn't believe it. She felt confident and happy about her new look.

Things were starting to look up, but Latrice wasn't following the plan that Kendra had mapped out for her in order for her to succeed. It turned out that Latrice never really went to school to begin with. She was able to get Kendra fake transcripts each semester to demonstrate she attended school and was on the Dean's list every semester. There was nothing that Kendra wasn't willing to do for her. On her 21st birthday, Kendra wanted to do something especially nice for Latrice. She felt it was reward that Latrice deserved because she had been doing so well in school.

On the day of Latrice's 21st birthday, Kendra decided it was time to get Latrice her own car. She went down to the local BMW dealership and purchased a brand new 325 convertible for her as a birthday gift, but more importantly she wanted Latrice to be around her friends when the gift was delivered to surprise her. Unfortunately, that day Kendra would receive the biggest surprise of her life instead. She went to the registrar's office to find out Latrice's schedule so she would know how to find her. To Kendra's surprise, Latrice was never enrolled as a student. She claimed she had been attending the school for the last two years. Kendra had even given her the checks to pay for her tuition every semester instead of sending the check out directly to the school. Kendra was pissed because Latrice had been lying to her. She was made a fool of and she didn't appreciate that. She also went to the former school where Latrice claimed she transferred from, but there was no record of a Latrice Simmons ever attending the school. Not only did she cancel the purchase of the car, she couldn't wait to lash out at Latrice when she got home.

A Crumbling World

Kendra's face was beet red when she walked into the house later that evening to find Latrice sitting behind the computer acting like she was doing research for a paper. On the way home from work she contemplated the best way to approach the situation. She knew she had to be straightforward and direct with Latrice. She was also pissed about the fact that Latrice had taken close to one hundred thousand dollars from her for tuition for the four years. Anger was written all over her face when she grabbed Latrice by the collar and started dragging her toward the family room. "What are you doing!?" Latrice yelled. "I want you to tell me what the hell you've been doing the last four years when you were supposed to be in school!" Kendra said angrily while tightening her grip on Latrice. "What are you talking about? I've been in school. You've seen my grades," Latrice attempted to stick to her lie. Kendra's devilish stare could cut right into Latrice. She had never seen that side of Kendra, but Latrice looked like an experienced former inmate who duked it out with the best of them in the prison yard. She knew she was caught and there was no way out of it. "I don't give a shit what you do, but you're going to give me back every cent that I gave you the last four years and you're gonna pack your shit and get the fuck outta my house," Kendra told her while still trying to tighten her grip on Latrice's shirt, near the collar.

"Didn't nobody ask you to wear your heart on your sleeve. You rich people always want something to feel good about. I didn't ask to be your charity case," Latrice told Kendra as she didn't care. Kendra couldn't believe how ungrateful Latrice had become. She damn sure wasn't going to allow her to disrespect her in her own house. "You're not going to disrespect me in my own house. Get the fuck outta my house!" Kendra yelled while attempting to push Latrice towards the front door. After about thirty more seconds of back and forth banter between the two women, Latrice's true self emerged and a fight ensued. "Get your fucking hands off me, bitch," Latrice told Kendra while swinging wildly. Kendra didn't have a chance to guard her grill. The punch landed right on her nose and blood started gushing out. When Latrice drew first blood, it was on. Kendra now had to defend herself. She snatched Latrice by the hair and started to punch her in the face. Latrice was on the losing end of the fight, but her defensive instinct kicked in just in time. She tackled Kendra to the ground, but unfortunately,

Kendra ended up hitting her head on a Marble statue standing in the corner of the room holding a spear in his hand. The spear went right through Kendra's head and she died instantly.

As panic started to set in, Latrice was contemplating the rest of her life behind bars because of the situation. "I'm not going to prison! I'm not going to prison!" she started to scream to herself. After sitting there holding Kendra's head in her lap while tears filled her face, she came up with a plan to assume Kendra's identity in order to keep her death from the authorities. Latrice didn't have much work to do as she had already been transformed by Kendra to look just like her. The fact that they were about the same size worked to Latrice's advantage as well. All she needed to do now was to take over Kendra's life. She decided to dig a hole that was about four feet deep and five feet long in the back yard to hide the body. Since Kendra lived in an exclusive neighborhood where the houses spanned almost five acres apart with 6ft high fences, it was easy for Latrice to wrap her body in a sheet and drag her to the backyard to bury her.

Stealing the identity of an established woman would prove to be a more difficult task for Latrice to handle. Kendra was well-known and respected by her peers in the community and at work. Latrice had to walk a fine line when she decided to undertake that new task. It had only been a couple of months since the physical transformation to look like Kendra had taken place. Few people if any had ever seen them out in public together. Latrice was now free to drive around in Kendra's cars, use her credit cards and take money out of her bank account. All those things were fun to do the first couple of weeks, but she had to start reporting to work soon.

When the firm started calling Kendra about an upcoming trial, Latrice was more than a little ignorant with her partners on the phone. She hadn't yet grabbed the professional and legal vernacular that Kendra was accustomed to and it signaled a red flag right away with the partners at the firm. Kendra was highly respected at the firm because of her professionalism, but when Latrice assumed her identity, it was like she had done a 180 degree turn. The day that she showed up to the law firm to announce she wanted to take a couple of months off because she had to deal with some personal issues was the day that all suspicions about her being fake was confirmed.

After Latrice left the law office, The FBI was immediately called by one of the partners who felt he knew Kendra better than Latrice could have ever pretended. After the FBI was alerted, the firm decided to grant

Latrice/Kendra the months she requested for leave even though she had a big trial coming up that she had no idea about. Another attorney was assigned because the firm stood to make a lot of money from that particular case. The new lawyer would request a new trial date until the issues with Kendra were sorted out. Latrice left that law office feeling secure that she had pulled off yet another stunt to take over someone else's life.

In Love with a Nut

Meanwhile, Kevin was all about Kandy. His world was filled with Kandy. He had no idea that the Kandy he was falling in love with was the most bitter Kandy he had ever tasted. There was nothing sweet about that Kandy and Kevin would find that out in a matter of time. As planned, he was filled with glee when he arrived in Miami anticipating the presence of his fiancée-to-be. Kevin was very creative as a person, which was one of the reasons he became a writer. He had planned the engagement all out in his head. I didn't really want to hear about his plans, but he forced me. I had to endure this whole shit for about fifteen minutes.

As told to me, Kevin planned to stay in a suite at the Delano Hotel in South Beach on the 12th floor, equipped with a spa and every kind of luxury imaginable. The 680 square ft suite was outfitted in white linen with nothing but European furnishings. Kandy picked him up in her convertible Benz as planned. Kevin was more than a little happy to see her. She was wearing booty shorts, halter top and high heels, the total opposite image of the average conservative doctor. His dick got hard the moment he laid eyes on her. Her creamy thighs kept him busy as she weaved in and out of traffic from Miami's airport to their destination on Collins Avenue. Even the valet had a hard time removing his eyes from the scantily clad beauty when she stepped out of the Mercedes Benz. Kevin got more than a few thumbs-up from the many admiring men who couldn't help glancing at Kandy. After Kevin and Kandy gathered their belongings from the trunk and the backseat of the car, they headed straight to the luxurious, $1300.00 a night suite to commence their rendez vous.

Besides the engagement ring, Kevin had stopped at the Gucci store to get a few items for his new love as well. Nothing was off limits and Kevin spent most of his pharmaceutical street earnings that week on Kandy. He didn't mind that. Kandy was impressed right away as they stepped through the door to enter the room. The plush down comforter, the all white look, the European décor of the room took her breath away. "What did I do to deserve this?" she asked him. Kevin let out a little smirk signifying how crazy he was about Kandy. She should've pursued acting in Hollywood because Kandy's performance was unforgettable, undeniable and convincing. "I want to give my baby a treat for treating me," she said with a flirtatious look on her face. She moved towards Kevin to unzip his pants so she could take his dick in her mouth, but he stopped her short and said, "We got this place for the whole weekend, baby. Let's take our time and enjoy this. I wanna get in the tub with you right now." I'm sure Kendra was thinking, *whatever Negro,* at the time, but she stayed in character and continued to play the perfect "I'm marriage material" type of girlfriend role. "You are so romantic. I can spend the rest of my life with you," she told him. As if Kevin's ego needed any more stroking. "I can spend the rest of my life with you too, baby," he said. All the plans he had worked out in his head went out the window when at that very moment, his impatient ass knelt down, presented the ring to Kandy and asked her to marry him. Of course, Kandy accepted his proposal.

Kandy went on and on about how much she loved the ring and how she was going to be a good wife to Kevin. Those words were music to his ears. He couldn't wait to marry the woman he was in love with. They both were in their birthday suits when they got in the hot tub. Kevin, however, couldn't hide his excitement. Like a good fiancée, Kandy reached for his Johnson and started massaging it in the warm bubble water. Her hands were soothing as she stroked his dick up and down hoping that her hand job would be enough to make him bust a nut. "You like that, baby?" she asked as she glided her tongue over her lips while giving Kevin a naughty look and stroking his dick. "You know I can't stand you like this. You're gonna make me bust if you keep doing that with your tongue," he pleaded. "Well, is it better if I use my tongue like this?" she said as she wrapped her tongue around his dick. The soothing warmth of her mouth was more than Calgon and Kevin was soon taken away. She sucked his dick for about five minutes before he announced he was coming. This time, Kandy did something that she had never done before. To solidify her performance, she swallowed every drop of Kevin's semen and then looked him and asked, "Do you like that?" Kevin's dumb ass couldn't wait to give her a response, "Hell yeah, baby. You can swallow this, too?! Dammmmmnnn!" Kevin was excited and he just knew that his investment in a ring for Kandy was the best thing that he ever did.

The blowjob in the hot tub was just the beginning. Kandy ended up fucking Kevin the whole weekend in every part of the suite. They barely left the suite to go anywhere. They watched television together, ate together, showered together and even joked with one another. Kevin was convinced Kandy was true to him and she was real.

Unfortunately, because Kevin was so wrapped up in Kandy that weekend, he never got a chance to open the piece of mail that was handed to him when he left my office. He and Kandy made plans to see each other again the following week in Boston. He was flying her in to stay at the Four Seasons hotel in downtown Boston. The hotel was the best choice because Kevin still lived with his Momma. Since Kandy wore Kevin out the whole weekend, he decided to rest while on his flight back home from Miami.

The Real Truth

Kevin came home a happy man. All he could think about was his life with Kandy. He couldn't figure out who to pick as his best man between me and Rammel. He thought we were both happy for him, but I was only holding my true feelings about his girl. I hated that broad and I couldn't wait for Kevin to figure her out. They say the truth usually comes to light over time, but I didn't have too much time on my hands. With Kevin talking about planning a lavish wedding and exhausting all his savings on a damsel he barely knew, I had to do something quickly. Since he came back from Florida, all he talked about was Kandy. Unfortunately, Kandy was not speaking so highly of Kevin. She called me a few times to tell me about her upcoming trip to Boston and how she was going to bring the tape of me fucking her to my wife if I didn't go back to Miami with her. "What about Kevin, what you're gonna do about him?" I asked her. "I know you don't think I really give a rat's ass about that bastard, do you? As a matter of fact, I'm sure he'll be very interested in watching his best friend fuck the hell out of his woman too. You already know he got a screw loose and if he sees this tape, you're as good as dead. You might as well pack your shit and kiss your kids goodbye because you're coming back to Miami with me," she said in a definite tone.

"What is your motive for doing all this shit?" I asked her almost in a sad way. I wasn't sad about me, but I was sad for her. "All of my life, I've never had what most people consider the perfect life. And I realized that sometimes you have to create the perfect life for yourself. It's not going to come to you. I want you in my perfect life, and I always get what I want," was all she said. There was absolutely no rhyme or reason to her action. Forget a full deck, this chick wasn't even playing with a half deck. I wondered why Plan B hadn't taken effect yet. So another piece of mail similar to the last one arrived for Kevin again, but this time we were in the office having a meeting. The delivery was planned perfectly. My receptionist knocked on the door to announce that she had mail for Kevin.

After handing the yellow bubble envelop to Kevin, she left and closed the door behind her. "What's that, another fan trying to get at you?" I enquired. Rammel started laughing and urged Kevin to open it. "It feels like some kind of CD or DVD. Unless they start videotaping themselves and sending it to me, I doubt this is from a fan," he said. I was sitting back and playing my nonchalant role like I knew absolutely nothing about the piece of mail. "Open it up. Let's see what's inside," Rammel suggested. Finally, Kevin tore open the envelope and pulled out a DVD with a note that read "Special for you" right on the DVD. "Special, huh? Your fans are getting out of hand, bro," I said in an amusing way. Kevin was laughing and started feeling himself a little. "You know how it is. I bring that heat and the ladies can't help themselves. Wait til I hit them with part two of my book. They're gonna go crazy," he said. "Man, let's just watch the damn DVD before you start feeling yourself a little too much," Rammel said. As a fellow writer, I could never check Kevin on his ego because it would appear as jealousy, but Rammel was always there to check him whenever he started getting out of hand. "Yo Ram, why you hatin,' son? You know I got the ladies on lock," Kevin said jokingly. "How about we watch the DVD first, then we can talk about how you got them on lock," Rammel said. Kevin tossed the DVD to me. I inserted it in the disc drive on my computer and then pressed play.

Rammel and I damn near had to use all of our strength to restrain Kevin and keep him from punching holes on the wall all around my office. Rammel, Kevin and I were all shocked as we watched Kandy sucking the hell out of some dude's dick. At least, I acted like I was shocked. "I'm gonna kill that bitch!" Kevin said in anger while trying to get loose from our grip. "Calm down, man. You're gonna let a chick ruin everything that you have worked so hard for? You can't let that happen, man," I said to him. "Man, fuck that! She ain't gonna play me and get away with it!" he yelled angrily. "Kev man, you gotta calm down so we can think this through. We ain't gonna get anywhere with you hollering. The chick ain't even here," Rammel said. For the first time in my life, since we've been friends, I could see pain in Kevin's eyes. As tough as Kevin was, he was on the brink of tears after he calmed down. "What am I supposed to do, Dave? I was crazy about that chick. She got my twenty-five-thousand-dollar ring on her finger, man. I'm supposed to just walk away from this shit? She gonna have to pay for this, man!" Kevin said through sobs.

Now I was starting to second-guess the plan that my uncle, Rammel and I had devised to help Kevin see through Kandy's act. The original plan wasn't supposed to be like that. Kevin was supposed to watch that DVD on his way to Miami before he saw Kandy. He was supposed to watch it at the airport while he was sitting in the waiting area to catch his flight. He wasn't supposed to get on the flight. He was supposed to turn back around and leave Kandy be. Our original plan failed miserably. Now we had an emotional wreck on our hands. I felt bad. I had to get Rammel involved in the plan because he cared just as much about Kevin as I did. We wanted to be there for him to support and comfort him. He had never let his guard down like that in front of us. Kevin became a weak man for love. I realized that we were all susceptible to that weakness because we have no control over our hearts. At least Kevin finally found out the truth.

Tragedy

Kevin may have gotten emotional when he found out Kandy was sucking more than his dick, but his street streak never disappeared. The streets lived in him and he couldn't get away from it. Kandy came to town as planned and Kevin acted as if everything was fine. He picked her up from the airport and took her to the hotel. Kandy continued with her act when she saw Kevin. She gave him all the affection in the world and he returned the favor. All Kevin wanted was his ring back and his dignity. The plan was for him to wait until she got in the shower to take the ring and leave. Ok, maybe he was also planning on smacking her around a little bit for being a slut, but that was his plan, not ours. Meanwhile, Rammel and I never revealed to Kevin that I was the guy on the tape. Unfortunately, stealing that ring would prove harder than we originally thought

Meanwhile, Kevin received an unusual call from the FBI he never anticipated. FBI agents had been tailing Kandy for weeks since she showed up at Kendra's job. They had confirmed she was Kendra, but they had no proof of what happened to Kendra either. They needed to catch, Shaquana,

AKA Latrice, AKA Kandy, AKA Kendra, a career criminal, in the act in order to charge her with murder. The surveillance team not only tapped Kandy's phone but they knew everybody she was in contact with. Not one to ever become a snitch, Kevin didn't want to talk to the FBI when they first contacted him. However, when they presented him with videotape evidence of more than enough drug transactions that could land him a lifetime in prison, Kevin decided he would cooperate. Also, Kevin wanted the ultimate payback against Kandy, so he decided to play ball with the FBI.

By then, Kevin already knew that his life on the street was over. With the cloud of a lifetime sentence hanging over his head, he knew he had to find a different way to finance his lifestyle. There was no way Kevin could continue to sell drugs on the Boston streets. Not only that, his cooperation with the FBI would take away his credibility. He was damned if he did and damned if he didn't. Kandy suggested that she and Kevin go fishing. Now the roles had switched, Kevin became the charismatic actor while Kandy took on the role of director, so she thought. She made the arrangement for Kevin to rent a speedboat down by Marina Bay in Quincy, Massachusetts and they would ride down the Cape to go fishing. Kevin was not a swimmer and had a fear for the ocean. At first, he wanted to renege on the deal, but the FBI kept holding the life sentence over his head and he had no choice.

As planned, a speedboat was rented. Kevin picked Kandy up away from the dock where he rented the boat. She didn't want anybody to see her get on the boat with Kevin. She wanted to make it look like he was alone. After picking her up near the shore, a few blocks down, they took to the sea like two explorers. They were in the middle of nowhere when Kandy suddenly asked Kevin to stop the boat so they could fish. Recognizing his fear and lack of swimming skills kept Kevin away from the ledge. He didn't want to fall overboard by accident. Kevin should have never mentioned to Kandy that he didn't know how to swim. However, in order for the FBI to catch Kandy in the act and charge her with conspiracy to commit murder, Kevin had to sit on the ledge. He reluctantly did that while keeping his eyes focused on Kandy. The plan was for Kandy to push Kevin into the water and the FBI would appear soon enough to save him and charge her with the crime.

The FBI underestimated Kandy and their plan almost foiled. Kandy never took the time to look up to spot the quiet helicopter hovering above about a half mile away. When she decided to charge Kevin like a linebacker to push him overboard, he held on while his feet dangled in the water. Pleading for help, Kevin kept losing his grip while Kandy was standing over him with a hand gun to secure the plan. "I'm sorry it had to end this way Kevin, but I don't love you," she said as she cocked the gun back and started pulling the trigger. The rocking of the boat in the water forced her to miss her target. By then the helicopter was above the boat while an agent was on the bullhorn screaming, "Put down your weapon!" Kandy looked up and decided that firing a few shots at the helicopter might force them to pull away, but the sharp shooting agent in the cab unloaded two shots in her body before she had any chance to let off one shot. Meanwhile, Kevin was damn near going under in the water before a tube was thrown down to him to keep him from drowning. Kandy never had a chance. She died upon arrival at the hospital.

Latrice

While everything that Kendra was doing to help Latrice came from her heart, Latrice on the other hand was just heartless. A former inmate from the Framingham State prison in Massachusetts, Shaquana had a baby face. After serving a ten year sentence for killing a girl while she was still a juvenile, Shaquana Brown assumed the identity of a girl who went missing in Boston a week after she was released from prison. Latrice Simmons was born when Shaquana got to a shelter after being released. She befriended a woman at the shelter who had lost her child to the Department of Social Services fifteen years ago while she was under the influence of drugs. The woman walked around with all the important paperwork regarding her child because she wanted to find her. She had a birth certificate, social security card and a picture of her daughter as a child. Shaquana saw the woman's pain as an opportunity to start a new life. She stole the lady's paperwork and moved to another shelter across town in order to assume the lady's daughter's identity.

A terror since the day she was born because her mother had experimented with too many drugs while pregnant, Shaquana was the epitome of a problem child. Like Kendra who sympathized with her, Shaquana had spent most of her life bouncing from one foster home to the next. She had been victimized by many people and in all sorts of ways. However, the one thing that Shaquana despised the most was men who took advantage of women. Having been raped multiple times by multiple men since she was as young as six years old, Shaquana carried a vendetta throughout her life. At school, the other children made fun of her because of her secondhand clothing and the fact that her foster parents didn't send her to school with the best hygiene. She had to learn to defend herself at a very young age because of the torment she suffered at the hands of her peers.

By the age of twelve, Shaquana had been raped and left for dead by a man in a dark alley. When she was miraculously found and brought to the hospital, her foster mother refused to accept her back into her home because she didn't want to deal with her trauma. Forced to be placed in a new home, Shaquana never really had time to adjust to a constant and stable environment. When she finally left the hospital a few weeks later, she vowed not to ever become a victim again. She started carrying a switchblade in her bag for protection and anybody who came close to threatening her got the wrath of her blade near their throats. Shaquana's new foster mother didn't have any pity on her. She was more into the miniscule amount of money that she received from the state monthly instead of the well-being of Shaquana. It was evident because Shaquana stayed out at all hours of the night and there was never any consequence to her action.

By the time Shaquana reached the age of fifteen, she was having sex regularly and she had developed a reputation for being loose. One day while she was out with a boy, he tried to force himself on her and she refused his advances. When he continued to press on, she told him to leave her alone. However, this boy didn't heed her warning. When he forcefully grabbed her by putting his hand around her throat, Shaquana had already pulled the switchblade out of her bag and it went about two inches deep across the boy's throat in a matter of seconds without any more warnings. The boy died upon arrival at the hospital. Since Shaquana was still a minor, she was sent to a juvenile detention center until the age of twenty-one. However, while at the juvenile detention center, she kept getting into fisticuffs with another girl. One day she waited for the girl near a bathroom to slice the girl's face with a razorblade. She received an additional five-year sentence for that incident, which she had to serve at the Framingham State Prison for Women. Since her sentence was served in succession, it never received any coverage in the media. Since her case was never discussed publicly in the media when she was a juvenile, it gave her a chance to start anew when she got out of prison.

Even at the age of twenty-five, Shaquana still looked like a teenager. She was able to become that teenager when she stole the identity of that woman's daughter at the shelter. With papers in hand as proof, Shaquana was able to fool the shelter as well as Kendra into believing that she was Latrice Simmons. She never thought that a new identity would give her access to a world she could have never imagined. It was one thing for Shaquana to steal the identity of a 17 year-old girl, but stealing the identity of a prominent woman was what got her caught.

Conclusion

Shaquana didn't even bother to investigate anything about the firm before she went in there. One of the partners in the firm was Kendra's lover and it was he who figured out that Shaquana was not really Kendra. The real Kendra always greeted him with kiss and a hug. They had an open relationship throughout the office, which was one of the reasons why some people were jealous of her. Also, Kendra was always on top of her cases and knew that the firm needed her despite her known flaws. When the other partner took a look at Shaquana's chest, he knew that wasn't his girl because Kendra's breasts were at least two cup sizes bigger than Shaquana's. After he alerted the FBI, they set up shop in front of Kendra's house and started monitoring Shaquana's every move. Special agent, Raymaond Barkley, AKA, Ray Ray was assigned to the case.

Shaquana was a loner, but she couldn't keep her antics to herself. The FBI had no idea what they were looking for because Shaquana looked so much like Kendra. No one had reported Kendra missing. There was no one that could point out that Shaquana was not really Kendra, except for the partner at the law firm. The FBI decided to shift their focus to find the real Kendra. Meanwhile, all the phones in the house were tapped, along with Shaquana's cell phone. The FBI knew her every move. They knew she was a criminal in every aspect of the word. She was going to be charged with blackmail, conspiracy to murder, first degree murder and a host of other charges. The FBI worked tirelessly to make sure they built a strong case against Shaquana, but it was Shaquana who gave them the ammunition to build a stronger case.

In the absence of Shaquana from Kendra's house, a couple of FBI agents went in and started looking through the drawers looking for any clue to could help determine whether or not Shaquana had something to do with Kendra's disappearance. At first, they didn't believe she was a criminal because she went about her day like normal affluent woman would. It wasn't until the agents found a diary that they realized that they were dealing with a crazed woman willing to do anything to complete a book that she wanted to write. She kept accounts of her sexcapades with Kevin as well as me and all the things she had planned on doing to destroy me and my family. My official title, according to the FBI, was Mr. Erotica. She gave me that moniker because my first book, *The Bedroom Bandit*, was an erotic book. Her goal was to destroy Mr. Erotica and emerge with a book that was twice as good with that same title. I also found out from agent Bradley that Kendra had put a drug called Rohytnol in my drink the very first time we met for drinks at the bar. The affect of the drug kept me conscious but I couldn't remember anything that I did, which was how she was able to videotape the whole sexual act in the beginning.

Perhaps Shaquana's plan would have worked if she didn't decide that Kevin had to be killed. She wanted to kill Kevin, but more importantly, she had plans to torture me once I made it back to Florida with her. She had a list of things she wanted to do to me to ensure a slow and painful death. She was upset that I was able to use so many women for my own gain and thought I could financially capitalize on it at the end. She wanted to teach me a lesson. When the FBI finally decided to go public with their report on the case, communities from Boston to Atlanta to Miami realized there had been a psychopath on the loose. Before she left to come to Boston, she wrote in her book where she had buried Kendra's body and how the whole incident took place. Kevin was more than a little relieved that the FBI discovered Shaquana's plans before she executed her plans. His non-swimming ass was definitely gonna go down.

The case actually ended up working out for the better. I got to keep my marriage intact. I was grateful everyday for my wife and told her how much I appreciated her every chance I got. My best friend was lured away from the drug game and I swore Rammel to secrecy about the whole thing. I never wanted Kevin to find out what really happened between me and Kendra because Kevin was so in love with her. I wished I could have gone to him like a man and tell him the truth. I was happy that Rammel was there as my support system while we figured out a way to get Kevin back on track. The three musketeers were back at work and this time we were planning to take over the publishing industry. Nobody really knew it, but I had a big dinner at my house to celebrate my friends and family. All the people who are close to me were present - my mother, my uncle, Rammel and his mom, Kevin and his mom, my wife and my kids and most of all God was in the house.

The End

It may not be Histeria Lane, but these desperate housewives are fed up with their neglecting husbands. Their sexual needs take precedence over the millions of dollars their husbands bring home every year to keep them happy in their affluent neighborhood. While their husbands claim to be hard at work, these wives are doing a little work of their own with the bedroom bandit. Is the bandit swift enough to evade these angry husbands?

In Stores!!

NEGLECTED SOULS

Motherhood and the trials of loving too hard and not enough frame this story...The realism of these characters will bring tears to your spirit as you discover the hero in the villain you never saw coming...

In Stores!!!

Jimmy and Nina continue to feel a void in their lives because they haven't a clue about their genealogical make-up. Jimmy falls victims to a life threatening illness and only the right organ donor can save his life. Will the donor be the bridge to reconnect Jimmy and Nina to their biological family? Will Nina be the strength for her brother in his time of need? Will they ever find out what really happened to their mother?

In Stores!!!

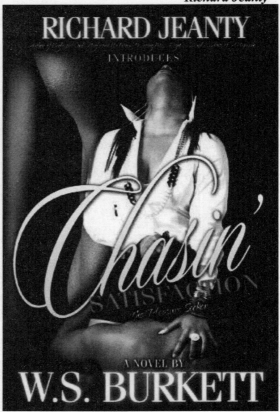

Betrayal, lust, lies, murder, deception, sex and tainted love frame this story... Julian Stevens lacks the ambition and freak ability that Miko looks for in a man, but she married him despite his flaws to spite an ex-boyfriend. When Miko least expects it, the old boyfriend shows up and ready to sweep her off her feet again. She wants to have her cake and eat it too. While Miko's doing her own thing, Julian is determined to become everything Miko ever wanted in a man and more, but will he go to extreme lengths to prove he's worthy of Miko's love? Julian Stevens soon finds out that he's capable of being more than he could ever imagine as he embarks on a journey that will change his life forever.

In Stores!!!

The police in New York and other major cities around the country are increasingly victimizing black men. The violence has escalated to deadly force, most of the time without justification. In this controversial book, noted author Richard Jeanty, tackles the problem of police brutality and the unfair treatment of Black men at the hands of police in New York City and the rest of the country.

In Stores!!!

Just when Darren thinks his relationship with Tina is flourishing, there is yet another hurdle on the road hindering their bliss. Tina saw a therapist for months to deal with her sexual addiction, but now Darren is wondering if she was ever treated completely. Darren has not been taking care of home and Tina's frustrated and agrees to a break-up with Darren. Will Darren lose Tina for good? Will Tina ever realize that Darren is the best man for her?

In Stores!!

Ronald Murphy was a player all his life until he and his best friend, Myles, met the women of their dreams during a brief vacation in South Beach, Florida. Sexual Jeopardy is story of trust, betrayal, forgiveness, friendship and hope.
In Stores!!!

Tina develops an insatiable sexual appetite very early in life. She
only loves her boyfriend, Darren, but he's too far away in college to satisfy her sexual needs.
Tina decides to get buck wild away in college
Will her sexual trysts jeopardize the lives of the men in her life?

In Stores!!!

Faith Jones, a woman in her mid-thirties, has given up on ever finding love again until she met her son's best friend, Darius. Faith Jones is walking a thin line of betrayal against her son for the love of Darius. Will Faith allow her emotions to outweigh her common sense?

In Stores!!!

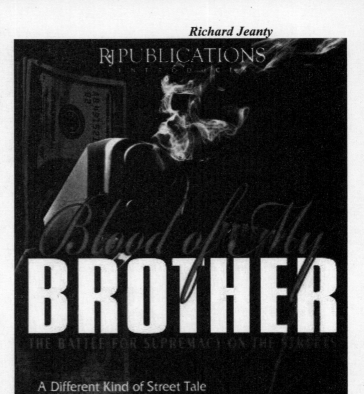

Roc was the man on the streets of Philadelphia, until his younger brother decided it was time to become his own man by wreaking havoc on Roc's crew without any regards for the blood relation they share. Drug, murder, mayhem and the pursuit of happiness can lead to deadly consequences. This story can only be told by a person who has lived it.

In Stores!!!

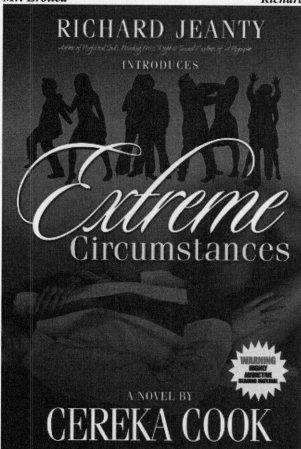

What happens when a devoted woman is betrayed? Come take a ride with Chanel as she takes her boyfriend, Donnell, to circumstances beyond belief after he betrays her trust with his endless infidelities. How long can Chanel's friend, Janai, use her looks to get what she wants from men before it catches up to her? Find out as Janai's gold-digging ways catch up with and she has to face the consequences of her extreme actions.

In Stores!!!

Violence, Intimidation and carnage are the order as Nathan and his brother set out to build the most powerful drug empires in Chicago. However, when God comes knocking, Nathan's conscience starts to surface. Will his haunted criminal past get the best of him?

In Stores!!

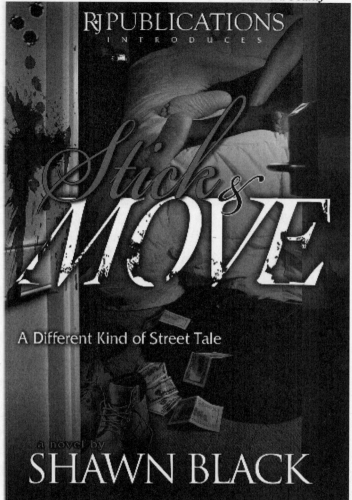

RJ PUBLICATIONS
I N T R O D U C E S

Stick &
MOVE

A Different Kind of Street Tale

a novel by
SHAWN BLACK

Yasmina witnessed the brutal murder of her parents at a young age at the hand of a drug dealer. This event stained her mind and upbringing as a result. Will Yamina's life come full circle with her past? Find out as Yasmina's crew, The Platinum Chicks, set out to make a name for themselves on the street.

In stores!!

Ashland's mother, Bianca, fights hard to suppress the truth from her daughter because she doesn't want her to marry Jordan, the grandson of an ex-lover she loathes. Ashland soon finds out how cruel and vengeful her mother can be, but what price will Bianca pay for redemption?

In stores!!

Malcolm is a wealthy virgin who decides to conceal his wealth From the world until he meets the right woman. His wealthy best friend, Dexter, hides his wealth from no one. Malcolm struggles to find love in an environment where vanity and materialism are rampant, while Dexter is getting more than enough of his share of women. Malcolm needs develop self-esteem and confidence to meet the right woman and Dexter's confidence is borderline arrogance.
Will bad boys like Dexter continue to take women for a ride?

Or will nice guys like Malcolm continue to finish last?

In Stores!!!

What happens when a woman's devotion to her fiancee is tested weeks before she gets married? What if her fiancee is just hiding behind the veil of ministry to deceive her? Find out as Sean Mitchell takes you on a journey you'll never forget into the lives of Angelica, Titus and Aurelius.

In Stores!!

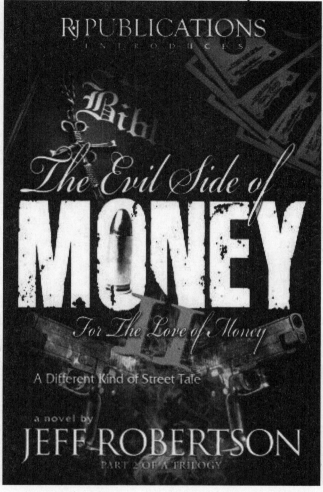

A beautigul woman from Bolivia threatens the existence of the drug empire that Nate and G have built. While Nate is head over heels for her, G can see right through her. As she brings on more conflict between the crew, G sets out to show Nate exactly who she is before she brings about their demise.

In Stores!!!

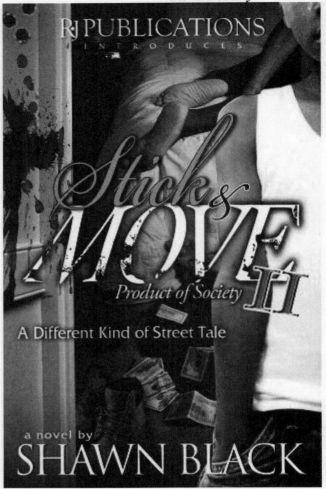

Scorcher and Yasmina's low key lifestyle was interrupted when they were taken down by the Feds, but their daughter, Serosa, was left to be raised by the foster care system. Will Serosa become a product of her environment or will she rise above it all? Her bloodline is undeniable, but will she be able to control it?

In Stores!!

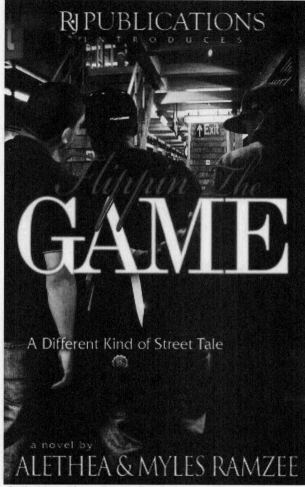

An ex-drug dealer finds himself in a bind after he's caught by the Feds. He has to decide which is more important, his family or his loyalty to the game. As he fights hard to make a decision, those who helped him to the top fear the worse from him. Will he get the chance to tell the govt. whole story, or will someone get to him before he becomes a snitch?

In Stores!!!

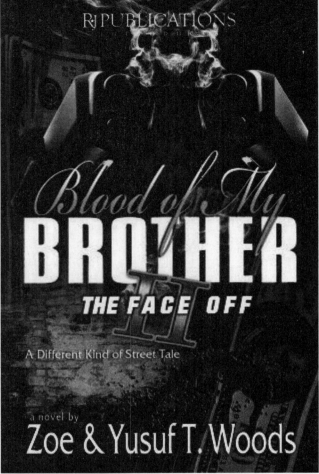

What will Roc do when he finds out the true identity of Solo? Will the blood shed come from his own brother Lil Mac? Will Roc and Solo take their beef to an explosive height on the street? Find out as Zoe and Yusuf bring the second installment to their hot street joint, Blood of My Brother.

In Stores!!!

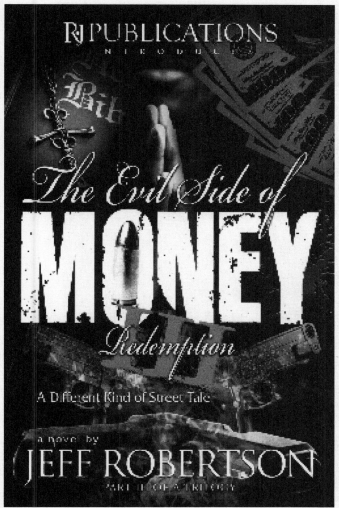

Forced to abandon the drug world for good, Nathan and G attempt to change their lives and move forward, but will their past come back to haunt them? This final installment will leave you speechless.

Coming November 2009

Nafys Muhammad managed to beat the charges in court, but
will he beat them on the street? There will be many
revelations in this story as betrayal, greed, sex scandal
corruption and murder unravels throughout every page. Get
ready for a rough ride.

Coming December 2009

Deon is at the mercy of a ruthless gang that kidnapped him. In a foreign land where he knows nothing about the culture, he has to use his survival instincts and his wit to outsmart his captors. Will the Hoodfellas show up in time to rescue Deon, or will Crazy D take over once again and fight an all out war by himself?

Coming March 2010

While Yasmina sits on death row awaiting her fate, her daughter, Serosa, is fighting the fight of her life on the outside. Her genetic structure that indirectly bins her to her parents could also be her downfall and force her to see that there's no way out!

Coming January 2010

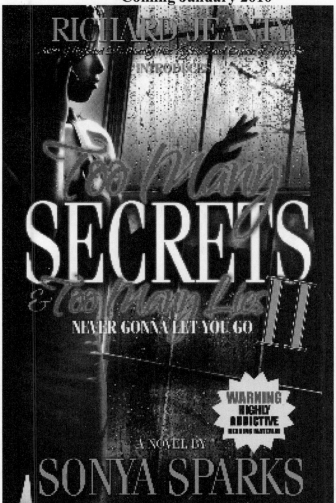

The drama continues as Deshun is hunted by Angela who still feels that ex-girlfriend Kayla is still trying to win his heart, though he brutally raped her. Angela will kill anyone who gets in her way, but is DeShun worth all the aggravation?

Coming September 2009

Buck Johnson was forced to make the best out of worst situation. He has witnessed the most cruel events in his life and it is those events who the man that he has become. Was the Johnson family ignorant souls through no fault of their own?

Coming October 2009

When an Ex-con finds himself destitute and in dire need of the basic necessities after he's released from prison, he turns to what he knows best, crime, but at what cost? Extortion, murder and mayhem drives him back to the top, but will he stay there?

In Stores !!!

What happens when someone falls insanely in love?
Stalking is just the beginning.
In Stores!!!

My Partner's Wife
In this twisted tale of seduction, Marcus Williams finds himself taking refuge in the arms of a woman completely forbidden to him after he discovered his cheating fiancee s sexual trysts. His life spirals out of control after the death of his partner while the killer is still on the loose. Marcus is conflicted about his decision to honor his partner or to completely allow his heart to decide his fate. Always the sucker for love, Marcus starts to fall head over heels for his partner s wife. However, with more deaths on the horizon, Marcus may soon find himself serving time with the same convicts he had been putting behind bars.

In Stores November 2010

Deceived
Rhasan Jones was given a second chance at life when he moved from his slum ridden North Carolina neighborhood to Newport News, VA to live with his grandparents. It didn't take long for him to figure out all the ghettos in America were just the same. After being introduced to a crack epidemic sweeping the nation, he met Cross, a crazed New Yorker who would stop at nothing for his thirst for life's finer things...

In Stores December 2010

Going all Out
When Pharoah megtg Tez, he thought he was helping by putting him on. But he never anticipated that tez would turn to a lunatic. A blood thirty dude, Tez kills at will with no regard for life and no one is off limits. Pharoah now has to watch his back because Tez is out of control...

In Stores January 2011

Hoodfellas III
Deon and his crew are forced to return back to the States. However, lurking in Deon's mind is revenge for the death of his fallen crewmembers. This personal

vendetta has to be settled before Deon and the Hoodfellas can have peace of mind, but at what price will revenge come?

In Stores March 2011

Use this coupon to order by mail
1. Neglected Souls, Richard Jeanty $14.95 Available
2. Neglected No More, Richard Jeanty $14.95 Avail
3. Ignorant Souls, Richard Jeanty $15.00, Available
4. Sexual Exploits of Nympho, Richard Jeanty $14.95 Available
5. Meeting Ms. Right's Whip Appeal, Richard Jeanty $14.95
6. Me and Mrs. Jones, K.M Thompson $14.95Available
7. Chasin' Satisfaction, W.S Burkett $14.95 Available
8. Extreme Circumstances, Cereka Cook $14.95 Available
9. The Most Dangerous Gang In America, R. Jeanty $15.00 Avail.
10. Sexual Exploits of a Nympho II, Richard Jeanty $15.00 Avail.
11. Sexual Jeopardy, Richard Jeanty $14.95 Available
12. Too Many Secrets, Too Many Lies, Sonya Sparks $15.00 Avail
13. Stick And Move, Shawn Black $15.00 Available
14. Evil Side Of Money, Jeff Robertson $15.00 Available
15. Evil Side Of Money II, Jeff Robertson $15.00 Available
16. Evil Side Of Money III, Jeff Robertson $15.00Available
17. Flippin' The Game, Alethea and M. Ramzee, $15.00 Available
18. Flippin' The Game II, Alethea and M. Ramzee, $15.00 Available
19. Cater To Her, W.S Burkett $15.00 Available
20. Blood of My Brother I, Zoe & Yusuf Woods $15.00 Avail.
21. Blood of my Brother II, Zoe & Ysuf Woods $15.00 Avail.
22. Hoodfellas, Richard Jeanty $15.00 available
23. Hoodfellas II, Richard Jeanty, $15.00 Available
24. The Bedroom Bandit, Richard Jeanty $15.00 Available
25. Mr. Erotica, Richard Jeanty, $15.00, Available
26. Stick N Move II, Shawn Black $15.00 Available
27. Stick N Move III, Shawn Black $15.00 Available
28. Miami Noire, W.S. Burkett $15.00 Available
29. Insanely In Love, Cereka Cook $15.00 Available
30. Blood of My Brother III, Zoe & Yusuf Woods Available
31. My partner's wife 11/2010
32. Deceived 12/2010
33. Going All Out 01/2011
34. Hoodfellas III 03/2011

Name_____
Address_____
City_____State_____Zip Code_____

Please send novels circled above; Shipping and Handling: Free
Total Number of Books_____
Total Amount Due_____
        Buy 3 books and get 1 free. Allow 2-3 weeks for delivery
Send institution check or money order (no cash or CODs) to:
RJ Publications
PO Box 300771
Jamaica, NY 11434

Use this coupon to order by mail
35. Neglected Souls, Richard Jeanty $14.95 Available
36. Neglected No More, Richard Jeanty $14.95 Avail
37. Ignorant Souls, Richard Jeanty $15.00, Available
38. Sexual Exploits of Nympho, Richard Jeanty $14.95 Available
39. Meeting Ms. Right's Whip Appeal, Richard Jeanty $14.95
40. Me and Mrs. Jones, K.M Thompson $14.95 Available
41. Chasin' Satisfaction, W.S Burkett $14.95 Available
42. Extreme Circumstances, Cereka Cook $14.95 Available
43. The Most Dangerous Gang In America, R. Jeanty $15.00 Avail.
44. Sexual Exploits of a Nympho II, Richard Jeanty $15.00 Avail.
45. Sexual Jeopardy, Richard Jeanty $14.95 Available
46. Too Many Secrets, Too Many Lies, Sonya Sparks $15.00 Avail
47. Stick And Move, Shawn Black $15.00 Available
48. Evil Side Of Money, Jeff Robertson $15.00 Available
49. Evil Side Of Money II, Jeff Robertson $15.00 Available
50. Evil Side Of Money III, Jeff Robertson $15.00 Available
51. Flippin' The Game, Alethea and M. Ramzee, $15.00 Available
52. Flippin' The Game II, Alethea and M. Ramzee, $15.00 Available
53. Cater To Her, W.S Burkett $15.00 Available
54. Blood of My Brother I, Zoe & Yusuf Woods $15.00 Avail.
55. Blood of my Brother II, Zoe & Ysuf Woods $15.00 Avail.
56. Hoodfellas, Richard Jeanty $15.00 available
57. Hoodfellas II, Richard Jeanty, $15.00 Available
58. The Bedroom Bandit, Richard Jeanty $15.00 Available
59. Mr. Erotica, Richard Jeanty, $15.00, Available
60. Stick N Move II, Shawn Black $15.00 Available
61. Stick N Move III, Shawn Black $15.00 Available
62. Miami Noire, W.S. Burkett $15.00 Available
63. Insanely In Love, Cereka Cook $15.00 Available
64. Blood of My Brother III, Zoe & Yusuf Woods Available
65. My partner's wife 11/2010
66. Deceived 12/2010
67. Going All Out 01/2011
68. Hoodfellas III 03/2011

Name_____

Address_____

City_____State_____Zip Code_____

Please send novels circled above; Shipping and Handling: Free
Total Number of Books_____
Total Amount Due_____
          Buy 3 books and get 1 free. Allow 2-3 weeks for delivery
Send institution check or money order (no cash or CODs) to:
RJ Publications
PO Box 300771
Jamaica, NY 11434